How to . . .

get the most from your
COLES NOTES

Key Point
Basic concepts in point form.

Close Up
*Additional hints, notes, tips
or background information.*

Watch Out!
*Areas where problems
frequently occur.*

Quick Tip
*Concise ideas to help you
learn what you need to know.*

Remember This!
*Essential material for
mastery of the topic.*

COLES NOTES

Getting Along in . . .

German

For travellers

and students

Useful phrases

with pronunciations

Travel & culture tips

COLES NOTES have been an indispensable aid to students on five continents since 1948.

COLES NOTES now offer titles on a wide range of general interest topics as well as traditional academic subject areas and individual literary works. All COLES NOTES are written by experts in their fields and reviewed for accuracy by independent authorities and the Coles Editorial Board.

COLES NOTES provide clear, concise explanations of their subject areas. Proper use of COLES NOTES will result in a broader understanding of the topic being studied. For academic subjects, Coles Notes are an invaluable aid for study, review and exam preparation. For literary works, COLES NOTES provide interesting interpretations and evaluations which supplement the text but are not intended as a substitute for reading the text itself. Use of the NOTES will serve not only to clarify the material being studied, but should enhance the reader's enjoyment of the topic.

© Copyright 1999 and Published by
COLES PUBLISHING. A division of Prospero Books
Toronto - Canada
Printed in Canada

Cataloguing in Publication Data
Torlee, Jurgen, 1943–
Getting along in—German: for travelers and students,
useful phrases with pronunciations, travel & culture tips
(Coles notes)
ISBN 0-7740-0576-9

1. German language—Conversation and phrase books—English.
I. Title.   II. Series.

PF3121.T67 1998   438.3'421   C98-931014-0

Publisher: Nigel Berrisford
Editing: Paul Kropp Communications
Book design and layout: Karen Petherick, Markham, Ontario

Manufactured by Webcom Limited
Cover finish: Webcom's Exclusive DURACOAT

Contents

Getting Along in German
Introduction

Getting Along in German is a phrase book that will allow travellers
to all German-speaking countries in Europe to communicate more
easily. It should help you gain a greater appreciation and understanding of the countries and people (*Land und Leute*) you are
visiting.

The material is organized by themes and covers situations a
traveller is likely to encounter. Each theme starts with some general
information and is followed by a situational dialogue that serves as
an example of what you might hear and say. A list of useful phrases
and a mini-dictionary are included to facilitate conversations.

Special care is given to provide general information about
Germany, Austria and Switzerland and to make the traveller aware
of some of the cultural differences that exist between these cultures
and ours in Canada.

German in a nutshell

Here's a list of the most basic expressions in German, well worth memorizing on your plane flight.

Hello	(Guten) Tag (formal/informal)	(**goo**-ten) tahk
Good morning (day)	Guten Morgen	**goo**-ten **mor**-gen
Good evening	Guten Abend	**goo**-ten **aa**-behnt
Goodbye	Auf Wiedersehen	owf **vee**-dehr-zay-en
Yes/No	Ja/Nein	yah/nine
Okay	Okay	okay
Please	Bitte	**bit**-teh
Thank you (very much)	Danke (sehr)	**dahn**-keh (zehr)
You're welcome	Bitte/gern geschehen	**bit**-teh/gehrn geh-**sheh**-en
Excuse me	Entschuldigen Sie bitte/ Verzeihung	ehnt-**shool**-dee-gen zee **bit**-teh/fehr-**tsy**-ung
I'm Canadian	Ich bin Kanadier(in)	ikh bin cah-nah-dee-ehr/in
Do you speak English?	Sprechen Sie Englisch	**shprekh**-en see **ehng**-lish
I don't speak German	Ich spreche kein Deutsch	ikh **shprekh**-eh kine doytsh
I didn't understand	Ich habe Sie nicht verstanden	ikh haa-beh zee nikht fehr-**shtahn**-den
What is this in German?	Wie heißt das auf Deutsch?	vee hicet dahs owf doytsh
My name is...	Ich heiße...	ikh **hice**-eh
Where is...?	Wo ist...	voh ist

CHAPTER ONE

A pronunciation guide

We are following the standard High German pronunciation which is accepted among educated German speakers in Germany, Austria, Switzerland and Luxembourg. Although there are many different dialects spoken throughout these countries, they will probably be difficult for you to understand. If you use the pronunciation suggested here, you will be speaking comprehensible German and will be able to make yourself understood anywhere in the German-speaking world.

Each German word or phrase in this book is written with its English equivalent and a phonetic transcription. The stressed syllables are all in **bold type**. Just pronounce the transcription as if you were reading English. Some German sounds, however, do not have an English equivalent so the transcription offered here is the closest possible approximation.

Here are some basic guidelines to help you through:

- German spelling is more consistent than English. Basically, it sounds the way it looks!
- German is a little more "clipped" and is pronounced more crisply than English. Germans don't run their words together and there are no drawn out vowel sounds (like the English *train*). Vowels are single, pure sounds, without any movement of the lips or tongue.
- Pay special attention to vowels. They determine the overall sound and are critical to making yourself understood.
- German sentence intonation – the way the voice rises or falls – is similar to English.

VOWELS

German letter	Approximate Sound in English	Phonetic	Example/ Phonetic Transcription
a - long	r<u>a</u>ther	aa	Vater (**faa**-ter)
a - short	c<u>a</u>t (between cat and cut)	ah	Mann (m<u>ah</u>n)
e - long	s<u>ay</u>	ay	leben (**lay**-ben)
e - short	b<u>e</u>st	eh	Nest (n<u>e</u>st)
e - unstressed	th<u>e</u> (between <u>e</u>h and <u>u</u>h)	eh	bitte (**bit**-teh)
er - last syllable	fath<u>er</u> (but barely pronounce the <u>r</u>)	er	leider (**lye**-<u>der</u>)
en, le, et	(similar to English)	---	geben (**gay**-<u>ben</u>)
i - long	t<u>ee</u>th	ee	ihn (<u>een</u>)
i - short	l<u>i</u>t	i	bitte (**bit**-teh)
o - long	v<u>o</u>te	oh	lodern (**loh**-dehrn)
o - short	l<u>o</u>st (between lost and must)	o	Post (p<u>o</u>st)
u - long	l<u>oo</u>n	oo	Mut (m<u>oo</u>t)
u - short	p<u>u</u>t	u	Mutter (**mut**-ter)
y	like in German <u>ü</u> (see below)	ew	mytisch (**mew**-tish)

Vowels modified with an umlaut

ä - long	h<u>ay</u>, like German long e	ay	sät (z<u>ay</u>t)
ä - short	m<u>e</u>t, like German short e	eh	hätte (**heht**-teh)
ö - long or short	sl<u>ur</u> is barely pronounced	ur	schön (sch<u>ur</u>n)
ü - long or short	st<u>ew</u>, or as in French s<u>u</u>	ew	für (f<u>ewr</u>)

Vowel combinations (diphthongs)

ai, ay, ei, ey	r<u>i</u>te, l<u>i</u>ce, <u>eye</u>	i...e or -ye	mein (**mine**) zwei (tsv<u>ye</u>)
au	n<u>ow</u>	ow	Laune (**low**-neh)
eu, äu	c<u>oy</u>	oy	heute (**hoy**-teh) Häuser (**hoy**-zer)
ie	m<u>ea</u>t	ee	liest (l<u>ee</u>st)

CONSONANTS

		English letters used as phonetic symbols	
f, k, l, m, n, p, t, x	pronounced in most cases as in English		
b (at the end of word or between vowel and consonant)	up, lap	p	gelb (gehlp) lobst (lohpst)
b (elsewhere)	like in English b, but	b	Bauch (bowkh)
c (before ä, e, i, ö)	see (rarely occurs in words of German origin)	ts	circa (tseer-kah)
c (elsewhere)	cat	k	Café (kah-fay)
ch (after a, o, u, au)	hard ch as in ugh, or Scottish loch produced in back of the mouth	kh	Loch (lokh)
ch (after e, i, um-lauts, consonants)	soft ch, as exaggerated h in Hubert, produced in front of mouth	kh	mich (mikh)
chs	lacks	ks	sechs (zehks)
d (at the end of a word)	hat	t	Rad (raat)
d (elsewhere)	like in English d, do	d	da (dah)
g (at end of word)	lick	k	Weg (vehk)
g (at end of word)	soft as ch, as exaggerated h in Hubert	kh	wenig (vay-nikh)
g (elsewhere)	hard g as in gag	g	gut (goot)
h (after a vowel)	silent as in hour	--	gehen (gay-en)
h (elsewhere)	have	h	haben (haa-ben)
j	yes	y	ja (yaa)
qu	k + v, kit +vat	kv	quellen (kvehl-len)
r	always guttural when stressed, r may either be trilled with the tip of your tongue as in a Scottish r, or gargled; when unstressed, like in western		Radio (raa-dee-oh) gestern (gehs-tern)

3

s (before or between vowels)	zoo	z	so (zoh)
s (elsewhere)	set, last	s	was (vahs)
sch	shy	sh	schon (shohn)
sp, st (the start of a syllable)	shoe, sh + p/t	sh	Stern (shtehrn) spät (shpayt)
ß	moos	s	laß (lahs)
eiß	mice	ice	heiß (hice)
th	tick, h is silent	t	Theater (teh-**aa**-ter)
tsch	lurch	ch	deutsch (doytch)
tz	mats	ts	Platz (plahts)
v	for (in words of German origin)	f	voll (fohl)
v	vista (in words of foreign origin)	v	Vase (**vaa**-seh)
w	vest	v	wo (voh)
z	lets	ts	Zug (tsook)

All those capitals!

Nouns in German always begin with a capital letter regardless of where they appear in the sentence.

They also come in three varieties –
masculine, feminine and neuter – but you
don't have to master this so long as you
keep *Getting Along in German* at the
ready.

CHAPTER TWO

The basics

GREETINGS

As in most European countries, German-speaking people shake hands a lot more than we do. This occurs *every* time you meet a person and say goodbye even if this should happen several times during the day.

Good morning.	Guten Morgen.	**goo**-ten **mor**-gen
Good day/afternoon.	Guten Tag/Tag.	**goo**-ten taak
Good evening.	Guten Abend.	**goo**-ten **aa**-behnt
Good night.	Gute Nacht.	**goo**-ten nhakht
Goodbye.	Auf Wiedersehen.	owf **vee**-dehr-zay-en
Goodbye (telephone).	Auf Wiederhören.	owf vee-dehr-hur-en
See you soon.	Bis bald.	bis bahlt
See you later.	Bis später.	bis **shpay**-ter
See you tomorrow.	Bis morgen.	bis **mohr**-gen
See you tonight.	Bis heute abend.	bis **hoy**-teh **aa**-bent
This is Mr./Mrs. or Ms./ Miss...	Das ist Herr/Frau/ Fräulein...	dahs ist hehr/frow/ **froy**-line
Pleased to meet you.	Sehr erfreut Sie kennen- zulernen.	zehr ehr-**froyt** zee **kehn**-nen-tsoo-lehr-nen
How are you?	Wie geht es Ihnen?	vee gayt es **ee**-nen
Very well, thank you.	Danke, sehr gut.	**dahn**-keh, zehr goot
And you?	Und Ihnen?	unt **ee**-nen
Also very well, thank you.	Auch sehr gut.	owkh zehr goot, dahn-keh

There is no German equivalent for the informal conversational "hello." Informally, the shortened form of *Guten tag — Tag —* is used. Depending on the time of day, one of the other greetings might be used instead.

APPROACHING SOMEONE FOR HELP

Excuse me.	Entschuldigen Sie.	ehnt-**shool**-dee-gen zee
Could you help me?	Können Sie mir helfen?	**kur**-nen zee meer **hehl**-fen
Do you speak English?	Sprechen Sie Englisch?	**shprekh**-en zee **ehng**-lish
Do you understand English?	Verstehen Sie Englisch?	fehr-**shtay**-en zee **ehng**-lish
Yes/no.	Ja/nein.	yaa/nine
I'm sorry.	Es tut mir leid.	ehs toot meer lite
I don't speak any/ only little German	Ich spreche kein/ nur ein wenig Deutsch.	ikh **shprekh**-eh kine/ noor ine **vay**-nikh doytsh
Repeat, please.	Wiederholen Sie, bitte.	vee-dehr-**hoh**-len zee **bit**-teh
Please speak more slowly.	Bitte, sprechen Sie langsamer.	**bit**-teh **shprekh**-en zee **lahng**-zaam-mer
What's your name?	Wie heißen Sie?	vee **hice**-en zee
My name is...	Ich heiße...	ikh **hice**-eh...
What do you call this in German?	Wie heißt dies/das auf Deutsch	vee hicet daas owf doytch
Would you write that down, please?	Würden Sie das bitte aufschreiben?	**vur**-dehn zee dahs **bit**-teh **owf**-shri-ben
Spell it, please.	Buchstabieren Sie es, bitte.	**bookh**-shtah-**bee**-ren zee ehs, **bit**-teh
What does that mean?	Was bedeutet das?	vahs bay-**doy**-tet dahs
Okay, agreed.	In Ordnung.	in **ort**-nung
Of course/That's right.	Sicher/Das stimmt.	zikh-er/dahs shtimt
Thank you very much.	Vielen Dank.	**fee**-len dahnk

QUESTION WORDS

Who	Wer	vehr
Whom	Wem	vehm
What	Was	vahs
Why	Warum	vah-**room**
When	Wann	vahn
Where	Wo	voh
Where to	Wohin	voh-**hin**
Where from	Woher	voh-**hayr**
Which	Welcher/Welche/Welches	**vehl**-kher/**vehl**-kheh/
		vehl-khes
How	Wie	vee
How far	Wie weit	vee vite
How many	Wie viele	vee **fee**-leh
How much does it cost?	Wieviel kostet das?	**vee**-feel **kos**-teht dahs

NUMBERS

To make the most of your stay in German-speaking countries, learn how to count. It will save you time and money.

zero	null	nul
one	eins	ines
two	zwei	tsvye
three	drei	drye
four	vier	feer
five	fünf	fewnf
six	sechs	zehks
seven	sieben	**zee**-behn
eight	acht	ahkht
nine	neun	noyn
ten	zehn	tsayn
eleven	elf	ehlf
twelve	zwölf	tsvurlf
thirteen	dreizehn	**dry**-tsayn
fourteen	vierzehn	**feer**-tsayn
fifteen	fünfzehn	**fewnf**-tsayn
sixteen	sechzehn	**zekh**-tsayn
seventeen	siebzehn	**zeep**-tsayn
eighteen	achtzehn	**ahkh**-tsayn

nineteen	neunzehn	**noyn**-tsayn
twenty	zwanzig	**tsvahn**-tsikh
twenty-one	einundzwanzig	**ine**-unt-tsvahn-tsikh
twenty-two	zweiundzwanzig	**tsvye**-unt-tsvahn-tsikh
thirty	dreißig	**drye**-tsikh
forty	vierzig	**feer**-tsikh
fifty	fünfzig	**fewnf**-tsikh
sixty	sechzig	**zekh**-tsikh
seventy	siebzig	**zeep**-tsikh
eighty	achtzig	**ahkht**-tsikh
ninety	neunzig	**noyn**-tsikh
one hundred	(ein)hundert	(ine)**hun**-dehrt
one hundred one	hunderteins	hun-dehrt-**ines**
one hundred two	hundertzwei	hun-dehrt-**tsvye**
one hundred ten	hunderzehn	hun-dehrt-**tsayn**
one hundred twenty	hundertzwanzig	hun-dehrt-**tsvahn**-tsikh
two hundred	zweihundert	**tsvye**-hun-dehrt
three hundred	dreihundert	**drye**-hun-dehrt
one thousand	(ein)tausend	(ine)**tow**-zehnt
one thousand two hundred	tausendzweihundert	**tow**-zehnt-tsvye-**hun**-dehrt
two thousand	zweitausend	**tsvye**-tow-zehnt
one million	eine Million	**ine**-eh mil-**yohn**
one billion	eine Milliarde	**ine**-eh mil-yaar-deh

DAYS OF THE WEEK

What day of the week is today?	Welcher Tag ist heute?	**vel**-kher taak ist **hoy**-teh
Today is...Monday.	*Heute ist...Montag.*	hoy-*teh ist* mohn-*taak*
Tuesday	Dienstag	**deens**-taak
Wednesday	Mittwoch	**mit**-vokh
Thursday	Donnerstag	**don**-nehrs-taak
Friday	Freitag	**freye**-taak
Saturday	Samstag/Sonnabend	**zahms**-taak/**zon**-aa-bent
Sunday	Sonntag	**zon**-taak

DATES

What is today's date?	Der wievielte ist heute?	dehr- vee-**feel**-teh ist **hoy**-teh

Today is the first of July.	Heute ist der erste Juli.	hoy-*teh*-ist *dayr* er-*steh* yoo-*lee*
the second	der zweite	dayr **tsvey**-teh
the third	der dritte	dayr **dreet**-teh
the fourth	der vierte	dayr **feer**-teh
the twenty-second	der zweiundzwanzigste	dayr **tsvey**-unt-**tsvan**-tseeg-steh

MONTHS OF THE YEAR

When were you here last?	Wann sind Sie zuletzt hiergewesen?	**vahn** zint zee tsoo-**letst heer**-ge-vay-zen
I was here in ... January.	*Ich war hier im ... Januar.*	*ikh vahr heer im* ya-*noo-ahr*
February	Februar	**fay**-broo-ahr
March	März	mehrts
April	April	ah-**pril**
May	Mai	mye
June	Juni	**yoo**-nee
July	Juli	**yoo**-lee
August	August	ow-**gust**
September	September	zehp-**tehm**-ber
October	Oktober	ok-**toh**-ber
November	November	no-**vehm**-ber
December	Dezember	deh-**tsehm**-ber

EXPRESSIONS OF TIME

two months ago	vor zwei Monaten	fohr tsvye **moh**-naa-ten
last month	letzten Monat	**lets**-ten **moh**-naat
next month	nächsten Monat	**naykhs**-ten **moh**-naat
monthly	monatlich	**moh**-naat-leekh
this month	diesen Monat	**dee**-zen **moh**-naat
tomorrow	morgen	**mor**-gen
the day after tomorrow	übermorgen	**ew**-behr-mor-gen
yesterday	gestern	**ges**-tern
the day before yesterday	vorgestern	**fohr**-gestern
in the morning	am Morgen	ahm **mor**-gen
at noon	am Mittag	ahm **mit**-taak
in the afternoon	am Nachmittag	ahm **nakh**-mit-taak

EXPRESSIONS OF TIME (CONT'D)

in the evening	am Abend	ahm **aa**-bent
at night	in der Nacht	in dehr **nahkht**
mornings	morgens	**mor**-gens
afternoons	nachmittags	**nahkh**-mit-taaks
evenings	abends	**aa**-bents
tonight	heute abend	**hoy**-teh **aa**-bent
tomorrow morning	morgen früh	**mor**-gen frew
all day	den ganzen Tag	dayn **gahn**-tsen taak
every day	jeden Tag	**yay**-den-taak
now	jetzt	yehtst
earlier	früher	**frew**-er
later	später	**shpay**-ter
before	vor/vorher	for/**for**-hehr
after/afterwards	nach/nachher	nahkh/**nahkh**-hehr
soon	bald	bahlt

THE FOUR SEASONS

When do you swim?	*Wann schwimmen Sie?*	*vahn shvee-men zee*
in spring	im Frühling	im **frew**-ling
in autumn	im Herbst	im hehrpst
in winter	im Winter	im **vin**-ter
every summer	jeden Sommer	**yeh**-den **zom**-mer
during the winter	während des Winters	**veh**-rent dehs **vin**-ters

THE WEATHER

How is the weather?	Wie ist das Wetter?	vee ist dahs **vet**-ter
It is...	*Es ist...*	*ehs ist*
hot	heiss	hice
cold	kalt	kahlt
windy	windig	**vin**-dikh
sunny	sonnig	**zon**-ikh
cloudy	bewölkt	be-**vewlkt**
cool	kühl	kewl
foggy	neblig	**nay**-blikh
splendid	herrlich	**hehr**-likh
horrible	scheusslich	**shoyss**-likh
warm	warm	vaarm

It is...	Es...	ehs
raining	regnet	**rayg**-net
snowing	schneit	shneyt
hailing	hagelt	**hah**-gelt
thundering	donnert	**don**-nert
lightning	blitzt	blitst
clearing up	klärt sich auf	ehs klayrt zikh owf

HOLIDAYS

Merry Christmas!	Fröhliche Weihnachten!	**frur**-likh-eh **vye**-nahkh-ten
Happy New Year!	Glückliches Neues Jahr!	**glewk**-likh-ehs **noy**-ehs yaar
Happy Easter!	Frohe Ostern!	**froh**-eh **ohs**-tern
Happy Holidays!	Frohe Feiertage!	**froh**-eh **fye**-er-taa-geh
Happy Birthday!	Alles Gute zum Geburtstag!	**ah**-lehs **goo**-teh tsoom geh-buhrts-taak
Congratulations!	Herzlichen Glückwunsch!	**hehrts**-likh-en **glewk**-voonsh

A LITTLE SMALL TALK

How old are you?	Wie alt sind Sie?	vee ahl tzint zee
I am twenty-three years old.	Ich bin dreiundzwanzig Jahre alt.	ikh bin **drye**-unt tsvan-tsik **yah**-re aalt
How are you?	Wie geht es Ihnen?	vee gayht es **ee**-nen
Do you feel cold?	Ist Ihnen kalt?	ist **ee**-nen kaalt
No, I feel warm	Nein, mir ist warm.	nine, meer ist varm
I am tired.	Ich bin müde.	ikh bin **mew**-deh
I walked too much today.	Ich bin heute zuviel gelaufen.	ikh bin **hoy**-teh tsoo-feel gay-**low**-fen
It is beautiful here.	Es ist schön hier.	ehs ist shewn heer
I am happy.	Ich freue mich.	kh **froy**-eh meekh
I regret that I cannot stay.	Es tut mir leid, dass ich nicht bleiben kann.	ehs toot meer lite dass ikh nikht **bly**-ben kahn

11

CHAPTER THREE

When you arrive

Since the former German Democratic Republic ceased to exist, a traveller now has easy access to a vacation land stretching east to the Oder-Neisse border with Poland and the Czech Republic. Border formalities with the countries surrounding Germany are often so easy-going that you only have to ask to have your passport stamped. If you are staying for more than three months in Germany or seeking employment, a visa is required.

CUSTOMS

After your passport has been checked and you have collected your luggage, you will notice that customs clearance is marked with a green arrow leading to: *Anmeldefreie Waren* (Nothing to Declare) and a red arrow leading to: *Anmeldepflichtige Waren* (Goods to Declare). Personal clothing and other items for personal use are usually tax-free, but goods such as alcohol and cigarettes have to be declared. Customs officers in most major airports in German-speaking countries have a good working knowledge of English, but if this is not the case, you may find the following dialogue and phrases helpful.

Clearing Customs

Customs official: Your passport, please!
(Zollbeamtin):   Ihren Paß bitte! (**ee**-ren paas **bit**-teh)
                   How long will you be staying in Germany?
                   Wie lange bleiben Sie in Deutschland?
                   (vee **lahn**-geh **bly**-ben zee in **doych**-lant)

Traveller: (Reisender):	A few days. Ein paar Tage. (ine paar **taa**-geh) Three weeks. Drei Wochen (dry **vokh**-en) One month. Einen Monat. (**ine**-en **moh**-naat) I'm passing through. Ich bin auf der Durchreise. (ikh bin owf dehr **durkh**-rye-zeh) I'm here on a business trip. Ich bin auf Geschäftsreise. (ikh bin heer owf gehs-**hehfts**-rye-zeh)
Customs official:	Where will you be staying? Wo bleiben Sie? (voo **bly**-ben zee)
Traveller:	In a hotel. Im Hotel. (im hoh-**tehl**) With business friends. Bei Geschäftsfreunden. (by geh-**shehfts**-froyn-den) I will be travelling through Germany. Ich mache eine Ferienreise durch Deutschland. (ikh **mahkh**-eh **ine**-eh **fayr**-yen-rey-zeh durkh **doykh**-lant)
Customs official:	Do you have anything to declare? Haben Sie etwas zu verzollen? (**haa**-ben zee **eht**-vahs tsoo vehr-**tsoh**-len)
Traveller:	No, nothing at all. Nein, gar nichts. (nine, gahr neekhts) Yes, a carton of cigarettes. Ja, eine Stange Zigaretten. (yaa, **ine**-eh **shtahn**-geh tsi-gah-**reh**-ten) Yes, a bottle of cognac. Ja, eine Flasche Cognac. (yaa, **ine**-eh **flash**-eh **con**-yac)
Customs official:	On these items you have to pay duty. Diesen Artikel müssen Sie verzollen. (**dee**-zen aa-**tee**-kel **mews**-en zee fer-**tsol**-len)

Traveller:	But these are gifts.
	Aber das sind doch Geschenke.
	(**aa**-ber daas sint dokh geh-**shen**-keh)
	They are for my personal use.
	Die sind zum persönlichen Gebrauch.
	(dee zint tsoom pehr-**zurn**-likh-en geh-**browkh**)
Customs Official:	OK. Have a pleasant stay.
	OK. Einen angenehmen Aufenthalt.
	(OK. **ine**-nen **ahn**-geh-neh-men **owf**-ent-haalt)

LUGGAGE, PORTERS AND CAR RENTALS

Porters are available in most major airports and luggage carts are provided in the baggage claims area – usually free of charge. All major car rental companies are prominently displayed and have someone who speaks English. But if for some reason you have to rely on your own German, the following phrases may be useful.

Where are the car rental agencies?	Wo sind die Agenturen zur Autovermietung?	vo zint dee ah-gehn-**too**-ren tsoor **ow**-toh-fehr-**mee**-tung
Where are the luggage carts?	Wo sind die Kofferkulis?	vo zint dee **kof**-er-koo-lees
I need a porter.	Ich brauche einen Gepäckträger	ikh **browkh**-eh **ine**-nen geh-**pehk**-tray-gehr
Please take my bags...	*Bitte, bringen Sie mein Gepäck...*	bit-*teh*, bring-*en zee mine* geh-**pehk**
to the taxi stand/bus	zum Taxistand/Buss	tsoom **tahk**-see-shtahnt/buss
to the U-Bahn/S-Bahn	zur U-Bahn/ S-Bahn	tsoor **oo**-baan/S-baan
to the luggage lockers	zu den Schliessfächern	tsoo dehn **shlees**-feh-khern
Please be careful with this suitcase.	Vorsicht bitte mit diesem Koffer.	**for**-zekht **bit**-teh mit **dee**-zem **kohf**-fer
How much do I owe?	Wieviel macht das?	**vee**-feel mahkht dahs
Thank you.	Danke.	**dahn**-keh
Goodbye.	Auf Wiedersehen.	owf **vee**-dehr-zay-en

14

SIGN LANGUAGE

CUSTOMS	ZOLL	tsoll
INFORMATION	AUSKUNFT	ows-kuhnft
WASHROOMS	TOILETTEN	toy-**let**-ten
MEN	HERREN	**heh**-ren
LADIES	DAMEN	**daa**-men
EXIT	AUSGANG	**ows**-gahng
ENTRANCE	EINGANG	**ine**-gahng
NO ADMITTANCE	EINTRITT VERBOTEN	**ine**-tritt **fehr**-boh-ten
BUS STOP	HALTESTELLE	**hahl**-teh-shtel-leh
TRAIN STATION	BAHNHOF	**baan**-hohf
ARRIVALS	ANKUNFT	**ahn**-kunft
DEPARTURES	ABFAHRT	**ahp**-faart
DEPARTURES (plane)	ABFLUG	**ahp**-flook
TRANSIT SYSTEM	TRANSIT ZUEGE	**trahn**-zit-**tsew**-geh

CHAPTER FOUR

At the hotel

If you are planning to stay in any major tourist area it is advisable to book in advance.

At other times you can get a **Hotelverzeichnis** (list of hotels) from the local **Fremdenverkehrsbüro** (tourist information office), which is usually located near the main train station. The tourist information office will also book a room for you.

Germany has three different categories of hotels and boarding houses designated as follows: F for hotels and boardinghouses with breakfast included; G for country inns and boarding houses with more meals included; H for standard hotels. Each category is rated I, II or III (adequate, good, very good). In Austria and Switzerland, hotels and inns are rated with one to five stars, similar to the French system where stars refer to the number of amenities and facilities.

The terms **Pension** and **Fremdenheim** indicate a boarding house, offering either **Vollpension** (full board) or **Halbpension** (breakfast and some other meal). **Hotel Garni** is the equivalent of bed and breakfast and the sign **Zimmer frei** indicates a room or rooms to rent. **Gasthaus** or **Gasthof** usually refers to a country inn, while **Rasthof** means a wayside lodge with restaurant, located near the **Autobahn** or a main highway. **Jugendherbergen** (youth hostels) are not as spartan as they used to be and are used not only by young travellers but by travellers of all ages. You may also investigate the possibility of renting a **Ferienwohnung** (furnished apartment) if your whole family is travelling with you.

AT THE FRONT DESK

Traveller:	I would like a double room with a private bath.
(Reisender):	Ich möchte ein Doppelzimmer mit Bad.
	(ikh **merkh**-teh **ine dop**-el-tsim-er mit baat)
	A single room with shower and toilet.
	Ein Einzelzimmer mit Dusche and WC.
	(ine **ine**-tsel-tsim-mer mit **doo**-sheh unt vay-tsay)
Receptionist:	How long will you be staying?
(Empfangsdame)	Wie lange wollen Sie bleiben?
	(vee **lan**-geh **vol**-len zee **bley**-ben)
Traveller:	I don't know yet for sure.
	Ich weiss noch nicht genau.
	(ikh veyss nokh nikht geh-**now**)
	One night. Eine Nacht. **ine**-eh nakht
	Three nights. Drei Nächte.
	(drye **nehkh**-teh)
	One week. Eine Woche. (**ine**-eh **vo**-kheh)
Traveller:	How much is the room?
	Wieviel kostet das Zimmer?
	(vee-feel **kos**-tet daas **tsim**-mer)
Receptionist:	With breakfast?
	Mit Frühstück? (mit **frew**-shtewk)
Traveller:	Yes, please. What time is breakfast?
	Ja bitte. Um wieviel Uhr gibt es Frühstück?
	(yah **bit**-eh. um **vee**-feel oor geebt es **frew**-shtewk)
Receptionist:	From 6:30 to 10:30 a.m.
	Von 6 Uhr dreissig bis zehn Uhr dreissig.
	(fon zeks ooa **drey**-sikh bees tsehn ooa **drey**-sikh)
Traveller:	May I see the room?
	Darf ich mir das Zimmer ansehen?
	(dahrf ikh meer dahs **tsim**-mer **ahn**-zay-en)

I like it/I don't like it.
Es gefällt mir/Es gefällt mir nicht.
(ehs ge-**fehlt** meer/ehs ge-**fehlt** meer
nikht)
I'll take it/I won't take it.
Ich nehme es /nicht. (ikh **nay**-meh
ehs /nikht)

Receptionist: May I see your passport?
Kann ich bitte Ihren Pass sehen?
(kahn ikh **bit**-eh **eeh**-ren pas **zay**-en)
Here is your key.
Hier ist Ihr Schlüssel.
(heer ist eehr **shlews**-sel)

Traveller: Please wake me tomorrow at 8 a.m.
Bitte wecken Sie mich morgen um acht
Uhr.
(**bit**-eh **vehk**-en zee mikh **mor**-gen um
ahkht oor)

CHECK IN AND DEPARTURE

My name is...	Mein Name ist...	mighn **naa**-meh ist
I have a reservation.	Ich habe reservieren lassen.	ikh **haa**-beh reh-zehr-**vee**-ren **lahs**-en
We have reserved two rooms:	Wir haben zwei Zimmer reservieren lassen:	veer **haa**-behn tsvye **tsim**-mehr reh-zerr-**vee**-rehn **lahs**-en
a single and a double.	ein Einzelzimmer und ein Doppelzimmer.	ine-tsel-tsim-mer unt ine **dop**-pel-tsim-mer
Here's the confirmation.	Hier ist die Bestätigung	heer ist dee beh-**stah**-tee-gung
I am checking out tomorrow.	Ich reise morgen ab.	ikh rey-zeh **mor**-gen up
Please prepare my bill.	Bitte machen Sie meine Rechnung fertig.	**bit**-te **maa**-khen zee **mine**-neh **rekh**-nung **fer**-tikh
The service and tax are included.	Bedienung and Steuer sind einbegriffen.	beh-**dee**-nung unt **stoi**-ehr zint **ine**-be-grif-fen

18

CHAPTER FIVE

Banking and money

BANKS

Banks in Germany are generally open Monday to Wednesday from 9 a.m. to 1 p.m. and 2 p.m. to 4 p.m.; Thursday and Friday from 9 a.m. to 1 p.m. and from 2 p.m. to 5 p.m. Banking hours in Austria and Switzerland may vary somewhat. Currency exchange offices, called **Wechselstuben** (**vehk**-sel-shtoo-behn) or **Geldwechsel** (**gehlt**-vehks-el) are often open outside the regular banking hours and can be found in most airports, major railway stations and the downtown areas of larger cities. You can also change money or traveller's cheques at most hotels, but banks invariably offer more favorable rates.

Major credit cards and Eurocards are now accepted at most hotels, restaurants and shops. If you are exchanging large sums, you should compare the rates.

CURRENCY

The unit of currency in Germany is the **Deutsche Mark** called **D-Mark** (**day**-mahrk) and abbreviated **DM**. It is divided into 100 **Pfennig** (**pfeh**-nikh), abbreviated **Pf.**

Coins: 1, 2, 5, 10 and 50 **Pfennige** and 1, 2 and 5 **Mark**.
Banknotes: 5, 10, 20, 50, 100 and 1000 **Mark**.

As with other currencies, the **DM** banknotes vary in color and size, corresponding to their denominations, which makes it easier to distinguish them. Each note features a portrait by the famous German Renaissance artist Albrecht Dürer.

The Austrian monetary unit is the **Schilling** (**shil**-ling), abbreviated S. and divided into 100 **Groschen** (**gro**-shen) abbreviated **g**.

Coins: 10 and 50 **Groschen**; 1, 5, 10 and 20 **Schillinge**.
Banknotes: 20, 50, 100, 500 and 1000 **Schillinge**.

The Swiss franc or **Franken** (**frahn**-ken), abbreviated **Fr.**, is the currency in Switzerland and is divided into 100 **Rappen** (rahp-pen), abbreviated **Rp**.

Coins: 5, 10, 20 and 50, **Rappen**; 1, 2 and 5 **Franken**.
Banknotes: 10, 20, 50, 100, 500, and 1000 **Franken**.

EXCHANGING MONEY

When exchanging currencies, three different rates are posted:

Ankauf (**ahn**-kowf) - the rate for buying marks, schillings or francs. This rate is higher, more favorable to you than Canadian or U.S. banks, so it would be to your advantage to exchange most of your money in Germany, Austria or Switzerland.

Verkauf (fehr-**kowf**) - the rate for selling a particular currency. The reverse is true here: the **Verkauf** is always lower than the **Ankauf** rate and, therefore, any leftover money should be exchanged after returning home.

Reiseschecks (**rye**-zeh-shehks) or traveller's cheque rates are slightly lower than cash rates. Remember to always carry your passport when exchanging traveller's cheques.

Most major banks in airports, train stations and cities allow you to withdraw money from a banking machine with your own banking card from your account at home, or can give you a cash advance on your credit card.

At the bank

Customer:	Would you please cash these traveller's cheques for me?
(Kundin):	Würden Sie mir bitte diese Reisechecks einlösen?
	(**vewr**-den zee meer **bit**-teh **dee**-zeh **rye**-zeh tcheks **ine**-lur-zehn)

| Cashier:
(Kassierer): | Of course. The exchange rate is...
Aber gerne. Der Wechselkurs ist...
(**aa**-behr **gehrn**-eh. dehr **vehk**-sehl-koors
ist)
May I see your passport, please.
Zeigen Sie mir bitte Ihren Pass.
(**tsy**-gen zee meer **bit**-teh **ee**-rehn pahs) | | |

Where is the nearest bank?	Wo ist die nächste Bank? bahnk?	voh ist dee **naykh**-steh
I'd like to change... dollars this cheque some traveller's cheques	*Ich möchte...wechseln.* Dollar diesen Scheck einige Reiseschecks	*ikh* murkh-*teh* vehk-*seln* **dol**-lahr **dee**-zen shehk **ine**-ni-geh **rye**-zeh-shehks
Will you accept...? my credit card a bank draft	*Nehmen Sie...an?* meine Kreditkarte eine Bankanweisung	nay-*men zee...ahn* **mine**-eh kray-**deet**-**kahr**- teh **ine**-eh **bahnk**-ahn vye- zung
Do you need identification? Where do I sign?	Brauchen Sie den Personalausweis? Wo unterschreibe ich?	**brow**-khen zee dehn pehr-zoh-**naal**-**ows**-vice vo oon-ter-**shrye**-beh ikh
I'd like to buy... German marks Swiss francs Austrian schillings	*Ich möchte...kaufen.* D-mark Schweizer Franken österreichische Schillinge	*ikh* murkh-*teh...*kow-*fen* **day**-mahrk **shvye**-tser **frahn**-ken **ur**-steh-rye-khish-er **shil**-ling-eh
Please give me... small bills large bills the rest in change	*Geben Sie mir bitte...* kleine Scheine große Scheine den Rest in Kleingeld	gay-*ben zee meer* bit-*teh* **kline**-eh **shine**-eh **grohs**-seh **shine**-eh dehn rehst in **kline**-gehlt

CHAPTER SIX

Shopping

In Germany, Switzerland and Austria shops are usually open from 9 a.m. to 6 p.m. during the week and from 8:30 a.m. to 12 noon or 1 p.m. on Saturdays. On the first Saturday of the month they are also open in the afternoon, and on Thursday evenings until 9 p.m. In smaller towns the shops may be closed for a couple of hours at lunchtime.

There are two big sales during the year: **Sommerschlussverkauf** (summer clearance sale) usually around the end of July and **Winterschlussverkauf** (winter clearance sale). Clothes are drastically reduced, between 50 and 70 percent. They are excluded from exchange, **vom Umtausch ausgeschlossen**.

You will pay a healthy **Mehrwertssteuer**, or value-added tax, on purchases made in Germany (14.5 percent), Austria (10 to 20 percent) and Switzerland (6.5 percent). On most purchases, you will get a refund of the amount you've paid by redeeming the value-added taxes at the airport before returning home. Ask the shopkeeper to give you the proper forms.

I would like to go shopping today.	Ich möchte heute einkaufen gehen.	ikh **mehkh**-teh **hoy**-teh **eyn**-kow-fen **gay**-hen

At the shoe store

Salesperson: (Verkäuferin):	What would you like? Was wünschen Sie? (vas **vewn**-shen zee)	
Shopper: (Kunde):	I would like a pair of sandals. I möchte ein Paar Sandalen.	

Salesperson:	(ikh **merkh**-teh eyn paar zan-**daa**-len)
	What size do you take?
	Welche Grösse tragen Sie?
	(**vel**-kheh **grew**-seh **trah**-gen zee)
Shopper:	Size 42.
	Grösse zweiundvierzig.
	(**grew**-seh **tsvy**-unt **feer**-tsik)
	I like them and they fit well.
	Die gefallen mir und sie passen gut
	(dee gay-**fahl**-len meer und zee
	paa-sen goot)
	No, thanks, they're not quite right.
	Nein, danke, sie passen nicht sehr gut.
	(nine, **dahn**-keh, zee **pah**-sen nikht
	zehr goot)
	I'll take them.
	Ich nehme sie. (ikh **nay**-meh zee)

LOOKING FOR STORES

I am looking for...	*Ich suche...*	*ikh zoo-kheh*
a ladies' clothing store/	ein Damenbeklei-dungsgeschäft/	ine **dahm**-men beh-kley-dungs-geh-shehft/
a mens' clothing store	ein Herrenbeklei-dungsgeschäft	ein **heh**-ren-beh-kley-dungs-geh-shehft
an art dealer	einen Kunsthändler	**ine**-nen **kunst**-hehnt-ler
an antique shop	ein Antiquitätengeschäft	ine ahn-tik-vee **tay**-ten-geh-shehft
a bakery	eine Bäckerei	**ine**-eh beh-keh-**reye**
a bookstore	eine Buchhandlung	**ine**-eh **bookh**-hahnt-lung
a butcher shop	eine Metzgerei	**ine**-eh mehts-geh-**ry**
a camera shop	ein Photogeschäft	ine **foh**-toh geh-shehft
a candy store	einen Süsswarenladen	**ine**-nen **sews**-vaa-ren-laa-den
a cheese store	ein Käsegeschäft	ine **kay**-zeh-geh-sheft
a china shop	einen Porzellanladen	**ine**-nen por-tsehl-laan-laa-den

23

a CD store	ein CD Geschäft	ine say day ge-sheft
a delicatessen	ein Delikatessengeschäft	ine deh-li-kah-**tehs**-sen-geh-shehft
a department store	ein Kaufhaus	ine **kowf**-hows
a drugstore	*eine Drogerie /Apotheke	**ine**-eh dro-geh-**ree/** ah-poh-**tay**-teh
a dry cleaner's	eine chemische Reinigung	ine-eh **khay**-mi-sheh **reye**-ni-gung
a flower shop	ein Blumengeschäft	ine **bloo**-men-ge-shehft
a grocery store	ein Lebensmittelgeschäft	ine **lay**-bens-mit-tel-geh-shehft
a health-food store	ein Reformhaus	ine reh-**form**-hows
a liquor store	eine Spirituosenhandlung	**ine**-eh-shpee-ree-too-**oh**-zen-hahnt-lung
a market	einen Markt	**ine**-en mahrkt
a newsstand	einen Zeitungsstand	**ine**-nen **tseye**-tunks-shtahnt
a shoe store	ein Schuhgeschäft	ine **shoo**-geh-shehft
a shopping centre	ein Einkaufszentrum	ine **ine**-kowfs-tsen-trum
a souvenir/gift shop	einen Andenkenladen	**ine**-en **ahn**-dehn-ken-laa-den
a sporting goods shop	ein Sportgeschäft	ine **shport**-geh-shehft
a stationer's	ein Papierwarengeschäft	ine pa-**peer**-varen-geh-sheft
a supermarket	einen Supermarket	**ine**-nen zoo-per-mahrkt
a travel agency	ein Reisebüro	ine **rye**-zeh-bew-roh
a wine shop	eine Weinhandlung	**ine**-eh **vine**-hahnt-lung

A **Drogerie** specializes in non-prescription drugs and toiletries, an **Apotheke** in prescription medicines.

GENERAL SHOPPING EXPRESSIONS

May I help you?	Womit kann ich dienen?	voh-**mit** kahn ikh **dee**-nen
	Womit kann ich Ihnen behilflich sein?	voh-**mit** kahn ikh **een**-en be-**heelf**-likh zeyn
What would you like?	Was wünschen Sie?	vas **vewn**-shen zee
Where can I find...?	Wo finde ich...?	voh **fin**-deh ikh
Can you help me?	Können Sie mir helfen?	**ker**-nen zee meer **hehl**-fen
I'm just browsing.	Ich schaue mich nur um.	ikh **show**-eh mikh noor oom
Where is the...department?	Wo ist die...-abteilung?	voh ist dee...ahp-**tile**-ung
Can you show me...?	*Können Sie mir... zeigen?*	ker-*nen zee meer...* tsye-*gen*
this/that?	das hier/das da?	dahs heer/dahs daa
the one in the window/display case	das im Schaufenster/ in der Vitrine.	dahs im **show**-fehn-ster/ in dehr vee-**tree**-neh
something less costly /cheaper	etwas Preiswerteres/ Billigeres.	**eht**-vahs **price**-vehr-teh-rehs/**bil**-lee-geh-rehs
something larger /smaller	etwas Grösseres/ Kleineres	**eht**-vahs **grew**-seh-res/ **kline**-eh-rehs

DECISION-MAKING AND PAYING

It's not quite what I wanted.	Es ist nicht ganz das, was ich möchte.	ehss ist nikht gahnts daas vahss ikh **murkh**-teh
Can you please exchange this?	Können Sie das bitte umtauschen?	**kur**-nehn zee dahss **bit**-teh **um**-tow-shehn
No, I don't like it.	Nein, es gefällt mir nicht.	nine, ehs geh-**fehlt** meer nikht
I'd like a refund.	Ich möchte das Geld zurückerstattet haben.	ikh **murkh**-teh dahss gehlt tsoo-**rewk**-ehr-shta-teht **haa**-ben.
Here is the receipt.	Hier ist die Quittung.	her ist dee **kvit**-tung
I'll take it/two.	Ich nehme es/zwei.	ikh **nay**-meh ehs/tsvye
Do you have it in stock?	Haben Sie es auf Lager?	**haa**-ben zee ehs owf **laa**-ger

Can you please..?	Können Sie...?	kur-*nehn zee*
order it for me	es mir bitte bestellen	ehss meer **bit**-teh beh-**steh**-len
send it to this address	es an diese Anschrift schicken	ehs ahn **dee**-zeh **ahn**-shrift **shik**-en
deliver it to my hotel	es ins Hotel liefern	ehs ins ho-**tell lee**-fern
Where do I pay?	Wo ist die Kasse?	voh ist dee **kah**-seh
How much is it?	Wieviel kostet es?	vee-**feel kos**-teht ehss
Can I pay with...?	Kann ich mit... bezahlen?	*kahn ikh mit beh*-tsaa-*len*
this credit card	dieser Kreditkarte	**dee**-zer kray-**deet**-kahr-teh
traveller's cheques	Reiseschecks	**rye**-zeh-shehks
Do I have to pay the value-added tax?	Muss ich die Mehrwertssteuer bezahlen?	mus ikh dee **mehr**-vehrt-shtoy-er beh-**tsaa**-len
Do you have forms for that?	Haben Sie Formulare dafür?	**haa**-ben zee for-moo-**lah**-reh daa-fewr

CLOTHING AND ACCESSORIES

Can you help me?	Können Sie mir helfen?	**ker**-nen ze meer **hehl**-fen
I would like a/an/some...	Ich hätte gern...	*ikh* heh-*teh gehrn*
a hat	einen Hut	**ine**-nen hoot
a dress	ein Kleid	ine kleyet
a scarf	einen Schal	**ine**-nen shahl
a skirt	einen Rock	**ine**-nen rok
a belt	einen Gürtel	**ine**-nen **gewr**-tel
a blouse	eine Bluse	**ine**-neh **bloo**-zeh
a pair of sandas	ein Paar Sandalen	ine paar zan-**dah**-len
a shirt	ein Hemd	ine hemt
a pair of pants	ein Paar Hosen	ine paar **hoh**-zen
a raincoat	einen Regenmantel	**ine**-nen **ray**-gen-**mahn**-tel
a coat	einen Mantel	**ine**-nen **mahn**-tel
a jacket	eine Jacke	**ine**-neh **yah**-keh
a cap	eine Mütze	**ine**-neh **mewt**-seh
a brassiere	einen Büstenhalter	**ine**-nen **bews**-ten-hahl-ter
a panty hose	eine Strumpfhose	**ine**-neh **shtrumpf**-hoh-zeh

I would like a/an/some...	*Ich hätte gern...*	*ikh heh- teh gehrn*
lingerie	Damenunterwäsche	**daa**-men-un-tehr-**veh**-sheh
a pair of socks	ein Paar Socken	ine paar **zoh**-ken
a sweater/pullover	*einen Pullover*	ine-*nen pul*-oh-*ver*
with...	*mit...*	*mit*
turtle neck	Rollkragen	**roll**-kraa-gehn
V-neck	V-Ausschnitt	**fow**-ows-shnit
long/short sleeves	langen/kurzen	**lahn**-gen **koort**-sehn
	Ärmeln	**ehr**-meln
no sleeves	ärmellos	**ehr**-mel-loass
a tie	eine Kravatte	**ine**-neh krah-**vah**-teh
an undershirt	ein Unterhemd	ine **un**-tehr-hehmt
underwear	Unterwäsche	**un**-tehr-veh-sheh
an umbrella	einen Regenschirm	**ine**-nen **ray**-gen-shirm
a swimsuit	einen Badeanzug	**ine**-nen **baa**-deh-ahn-tsook
swimming trunks	eine Badehose	**ine**-neh **bah**-deh-hoh-zeh
a dressing gown	einen Morgenrock	**ine**-nen **mor**-gen-rok
gloves	Handschuhe	**hahnt**-shoo-eh
a handbag	eine Handtasche	**ine**-neh **hahnt**-tah-sheh
pyjamas	einen Schlafanzug	**ine**-nen **shlaaf**-ahn-tsoog

Sizes and fitting

What size do you take?	Welche Grösse haben/ tragen Sie?	**vel**-kheh **grew**-seh **hah**-ben/**trah**-gen zee
I'm size 40.	Ich trage Grösse vierzig.	ikh **traa**-geh **grew**-seh **feer**-tsikh
I don't know my size.	Ich kenne meine Grösse nicht.	ikh **keh**-neh **mine**-eh **grew**-seh nikht
May I try on this dress/ these shoes?	Kann ich dieses Kleid/ diese Schuhe anprobieren?	kahn ikh **dee**-zes klyet dee-zeh **shoo**-heh an-pro-**bee**-ren
Where is the fitting room?	Wo ist die Umkleidekabine?	voa ist dee **um**-kligh-deh-kah-**bee**-neh
Is there a mirror?	Gibt es einen Spiegel?	gipt ehs **ine**-en **shpee**-gel
It fits very well.	Es passt/sitzt sehr gut.	ehs pahst/zitst zehr goot

27

It doesn't fit.	Es passt nicht.	ehs pahst nikht
Can you alter it?	Können Sie es ändern?	**kur**-nen zee ehs ehn-dern
That's too big/small/ long/short.	Das ist zu gross/klein/ lang/kurz.	dass ist tsoo grohs/kleyen laang/koorts
Do you have something smaller/ longer/ shorter/cheaper?	Haben Sie etwas kleiner/ länger/ kürzer/ billiger?	**hah**-ben zee eht-vahs **kline**-ner/**len**-ger/**kewr**-tser/**bil**-li-ger

COLORS AND PATTERNS

| I don't like this color. | Diese Farbe gefällt mir nicht. | **dee**-zeh **far**-beh ge-**felt** meer nikht |
| I'd like something in a different color. | Ich möchte etwas in einer anderen Farbe. | ikh **murkh**-teh **eht**-vahs in **ine**-er **ahn**-deh-ren **fahr**-beh |

Do you have this in...?	*Haben Sie das in...?*	hah-*ben zee dahs in*
beige	beige	bayzh
black	schwarz	shvarts
white	weiss	veyess
green	grün	grewn
blue	blau	blow (as in now)
red	rot	roht
brown	braun	brown
yellow	gelb	gehlp
pink	rosa	**roh**-zaa
grey	grau	grow (as in now)
purple	violett	vee-oh-**leht**
mauve	lila	**lee**-lah
turquoise	türkisfarben	**tewr**-kees-**fahr**-behn
light...	hell...	hehl
dark	dunkel	**dun**-kehl
greenish	grünlich	**grewn**-likh
reddish	rötlich	**rewt**-likh
with stripes	gestreift	geh-**shtryeft**
with polka dots	mit Punktmuster	mit **punkt**-mu-ster
checkered	kariert	kah-**reert**

Conversion chart for clothing and shoe sizes

Women's dresses, coats, suits, skirts

Canada/U.S.	4	6	8	10	12	14	16
Europe	36	38	40	42	44	46	48

Women's blouses/sweaters

Canada/U.S.	32/6	34/8	36/10	38/12	40/14	42/16
Europe	38/2	40/3	42/4	44/5	46/6	48/7

Women's shoes

Canada/U.S.	4.0	5.0	6.0	7.0	8.0	9.0	10
Europe	35	36	37	38	39	40	41

Men's suits/coats

Canada/U.S.	36	38	40	42	44	46	48
Europe	46	48	50	52	54	56	58

Men's sweaters

Canada/U.S.	XS/36	S/38	M/40	L/42	XL/44
Europe	42/2	44/3	46-48/4	50/5	52-54/6

Men's shirts

Canada/U.S.	14	14.5	15	15.5	16	16.5	17
Europe	36	37	38	39	40	41	42

Men's slacks

Canada/U.S.	32	33	34	35	36	37	38	39
Europe	41	42	43	44/45	46	47	48/49	50

Men's socks

Canada/U.S.	9.5	10	10.5	11	11.5	12	13
Europe	36/37	38/39	40/41	42/43	44/5	46/47	48/49

Men's shoes

Canada/U.S.	7	8	8.5	9	10	10.5	11
Europe	39	41	42	43	44	44	45

I need a pair of...	Ich brauche ein Paar...	ikh brow-kheh ine paar
boots/rainboots	Stiefel/Regenstiefel	**shtee**-fel/ray-gen-shtee-fel
running shoes	Turnschuhe	**toorn**-shoo-eh
sandals	Sandalen	zahn-**dah**-len
shoes with flat	Schuhe mit flachen	**shoo**-eh mit **flakh**-en
heels	Absätzen	**ahp**-zehts-en
shoes with high	Schuhe mit hohen	**shoo**-eh mit **hoh**-hen
heels	Absätzen	**ahp**-zehts-en
slippers	Hausschuhe	**hows**-shoo-eh

These are too...	Diese sind zu...	dee-**zeh** zint tsoo
small/large	groß/klein	grohs/kline
narrow/wide	eng/weit	ehng/vite

Do you have a	Haben Sie eine	**haa**-ben zee **ine**-eh
smaller/larger size?	kleinere/größere	kline-ner-eh/**grur**-seh-reh
	Nummer?	**num**-mehr
Do you have the	Haben sie die gleichen	**haa**-ben zee dee **gligh**-en
same in black/red	in schwarz/rot	in shvahrts/roht
cloth/leather/suede?	Stoff/Leder/Wildleder?	shtof/**leh**-dehr/**vilt**-leh-dehr

THE JEWELRY STORE

Many tour buses stop at famous diamond-cutting centers, such as **Idar-Oberstein** an der Nahe, to give travellers the opportunity to view the intricate work that goes into the cutting of diamonds and gemstones and to make purchases for themselves, family and friends. The **Schwarzwald** (Black Forest) is, of course, famous for its cuckoo clocks, and Switzerland for its watches.

At the jeweller's

Salesperson:	What would you like?
(Verkäufer):	Was wünschen Sie? (vas **vewn**-shen zee)
Shopper:	Please show me a necklace.
(Kunde):	Zeigen Sie mir bitte eine Halskette.
	(**tsye**-gen zee meer **bit**-eh **ine**-eh **hahls**-keht-teh)
Salesperson:	Here is a very beautiful necklace in gold.
	Hier ist eine sehr schöne Halskette in Gold.
	(heer ist ine-eh zehr shew-neh **hahls**-keht-teh in golt)

Shopper:	How many carats has it?	
	Wieviel Karat hat sie? (vee-**feel** cah-**raat** haht zee)	
Salesperson:	Eighteen and it is on sale for...	
	Achtzehn und es ist zum Ausverkauf für...	
	(**ahkht**-seyn unt ehs ist tsoom **ows**-fehr-cowf fewr)	
Shopper:	Yes, I like this one very much and I'd like to take it.	
	Ja, die gefällt mir gut und ich möchte sie nehmen.	
	(yah, dee gey-**fehlt** meer goot unt ikh **merkh**-teh zee **neh**-men)	

Please show me (a/an)...	*Zeigen Sie mir bitte...*	tsey-*gen* zee *meer* bit-*eh*
bracelet	ein Armband	ine **ahrm**-bahnt
brooch	eine Brosche	**ine**-neh **brosh**-eh
cufflinks	Manschettenknöpfe	mahn-**shet**-ten-knup-feh
earrings	Ohrringe	**ohr**-ring-eh
engagement ring	einen Verlobungsring	**ine**-en fehr-**lohb**-unks-ring
goblet	einen Becher	**ine**-en **behkh**-er
jewelry box	ein Schmuckkästchen	ine **shmuk**-kehst-khen
pin	eine Anstecknadel	**ine**-eh **ahn**-shtehk-naad-el
pocket watch	eine Taschenuhr	**ine**-eh **tash**-shen-oor
ring	einen Ring	**ine**-en ring
tie pin	eine Kravattennadel	**ine**-eh krah-**vaht**-ten-naa-del
wedding ring	einen Ehering	**ine**-en **ay**-eh-ring
wristwatch	eine Armbanduhr	**ine**-eh **ahrm**-bahnt-oor

Do you have anything in...?	*Haben Sie etwas in...?*	haa-*ben* zee eht-*vahss in*
gold	Gold	golt
platinum	Platin	plah-teen
silver	Silber	**zil**-ber
stainless steel	Edelstaht	**ay**-del-shtahl

Is it in gold or	Ist es in Gold oder	ihst ehs in golt **oh**-der
just gold plate?	nur vergoldet?	noor fehr-**gold**-et
Silver plate?	Versilbert?	fehr-**zilb**-ehrt
How many carats is it?	Wieviel Karat hat es?	**vee**-feel kah-**raat** haht ehs

Can you repair this watch/jewelry?	Können Sie diese Uhr/ dieses Schmuckstück reparieren?	kur-nen zee dee-zehs oor/dee-zehs shmuk- shtewk reh-pah-ree-ren
How much are you asking for...	Wieviel verlangen Sie für...	vee-feel fehr-lahng- en zee fewr
All that glitters is not gold.	Es ist nicht alles Gold, was glänzt.	ehs isst nikht ahl-es golt vahs glehntst

PHOTO SHOP

At the photo shop

Salesperson: (Verkäufer):	What would you like? Was wünschen Sie? (vas vewn-shen zee)
Shopper: (Kunde):	I would like to have this film developed. Ich möchte diesen Film entwickelt haben. (ikh murkh-teh dee-zen film ehnt-vik-kelt haa-ben)
Salesperson:	Matte or glossy prints? Matt oder Hochglanzabzüge? (maht oh-der hohkh-glahntl-ahp-tzew-geh)
Shopper:	Matte. How much does the developing cost? Matt. Was kostet das Entwickeln? (maht. vahs kos-tet dahs ehnt-vik-eln)
Salesperson:	Do you need another film? Brauchen Sie einen neuen Film? (brow-khehen zee ine-en noy-ehn film)
Shopper:	Yes, please. When are the pictures ready? Ja, bitte. Wann sind die Bilder fertig? (yah, bit-teh. vahn zint dee bil-dehr fehr-teekh)
Salesperson:	Tomorrow. See you tomorrow. Goodbye. Morgen. Bis morgen. Auf Wiedersehen. (mohr-gehn. bis mohr-gehn. owf vee-dehr-seh-en)

I would like a/an...	Ich möchte einen...	ikh murkh-teh ine-ehn
35-mm color film	fünfunddreißig Millimeter Farbfilm	fewnf-unt-drye-sikh mi- lee-may-ter fahrp-film
black and white film	Schwarzweißfilm	shvahrts-vice-film
color slide film	Film für Farbdias	film fewr fahrp-dee-ahs
daylight film	Tageslichtfilm	taa-gehs-likht-film

I would like a/an...	Ich möchte einen...	ikh murkh-teh ine-ehn
artificial light film	Kunstlichtfilm	kunst-likht-film
fast (high-speed) film	hochempfindlichen Film	hoakh-ehm-pfint-likh-en film
24/36 exposures, please	Vierundzwanzig/ sechsunddreißig Aufnahmen, bitte	feer-unt-tsvahn-tsikh/ zehks-unt-drye-sikh owf-naa-men, bit-teh
one/two prints of	einen Abzug/zwei Abzüge	ine-en ahp-tsook/
each negative	von jedem Negativ	tsvye ahp-tsew-geh fon yeh-dem neh-gah-teef
Do you sell...?	Verkaufen Sie...?	fehr-kow-fen zee
cameras	Kameras	kah-meh-raas
automatic	automatische	ow-toh-mah-ti-sheh
simple	einfache	ine-fah-khe
single lens reflex	Spiegelreflex	shpee-gel-reh-flehks
batteries	Batterien	bah-teh-ree-en
camera case	eine Fototasche	ine-eh foh-toh-ta-sheh

Do you sell...?	Verkaufen Sie...?	fehr-kow-fen zee
filters	Filter	fil-ter
lens caps	Objektivdeckel	ob-yehk-teef-deh-kel
Can you repair this camera?	Können Sie diesen Fotoapparat reparieren?	kur-nehn zee dee-zehn foh-toh-ah-pah-raat reh-pah-ree-ren
The film is jammed.	Der Film klemmt.	dehr film klehmt
There is something wrong with...	Mit... stimmt etwas nicht.	mit shtimt eht-vahss nikht

SOUVENIRS, HANDICRAFTS AND TOYS

Germany, Austria and Switzerland are famous for their souvenir shops and the multitude of arts and crafts each country and region offers. Items sold in Austria's **Heimatwerk** (handicrafts), for example, are all handmade and therefore each is unique and of the finest quality. You can get Alpine cowbells, as well as traditional dolls, carvings and toys. The inventiveness, variety and craftsmanship of German toys have long been held in great esteem. At Christmastime (from late November on), outdoor markets are set up in cities, such as Munich, Bern, Vienna and Nüremberg, to offer some of the most ingenious and elaborate toys and souvenirs made. Austrian and Swiss winter sports equipment are also well known throughout the world. But petit-point embroidery and porcelain in Austria and linens and organdies in Switzerland are also good buys. Don't miss the fabulous array of watches and luscious chocolates in Switzerland.

At the store

Shopper:	Can you help me, please?
(Kunde):	Können Sie mir bitte helfen?
	(**ker**-nen zee meer **hehl**-fen)
Salesperson:	Yes, of course, how can I help you?
(Verkäuferin):	Ja bitte, womit kann ich Ihnen behilflich sein?
	(ya **bit**-teh, voh-**mit** kahn ikh **eeh**-nen be-**heelf**-likh zeyn)
Shopper:	I don't want to spend more than ...on it.
	Ich will nicht mehr als...dafür ausgeben.
	(ikh vil nikht mehr ahls...dah-**fewr ows**-gay-ben)
Shopper:	How much is this music box?
	Was kostet diese Spieldose?
	(vahs **kost**-eht **dee**-zeh **speel**-doh-zeh)
	Then I'll take it.
	Ja dann nehme ich sie.
	(yah dahn **neh-meh** ikh zee)

What do you have in...?	*Was haben Sie an...?*	*vahs* haa-*ben zee ahn*
leather goods	Lederwaren	**layh**-der-vaar-en
glassware	Glaswaren	**glaas**-vaar-en
beer steins	Bierkrüge	**beer**-krew-geh
porcelain	Porzellan	port-seh-**lahn**
wood carvings	Holzschnittzarbeiten	**holts**-shnits-ahr-bight-en
cukoo clocks	Kuckucksuhren	**kuk**-kuks-oo-ren
embroidery	Stickereien	shtik-keh-**righ**-en
Swiss army knives	Schweizer Armeemesser	**shvight**-sehr ahr-**may**-mehss-ehr
Tyrolean hats	Tirolerhüte	tee-**roal**-ehr-hew-teh
Tyrolean pipes	Tiroler Pfeifen	tee-**roal**-ehr-**pfigh**-feh-en
wristwatches	Armbanduhren	**ahrm**-bahnd-oor-en

English	German	Pronunciation
chocolate	Schokolade	shok-ko-laa-deh
Are these little spoons genuine silver?	Sind diese Löffelchen echt Silber?	zint **dee**-zeh **lerf**-el-khen ehkht **zil**-behr
How old is this beer stein?	Wie alt ist dieser Bierkrug?	vee ahlt is **dee**-zehr **beer**-krook
How much is this little cup?	Was kostet das Täßchen?	vahs **kost**-tet dahs **tehs**-shen
Do you have dolls in peasant costumes?	Haben Sie Puppen in Trachten?	**haab**-en zee **pup**-en in **trahkht**-en
How much does this set of tableware (cutlery) cost?	Wieviel kostet dieses Eßbesteck?	**vee**-feel **kost**-et **deez**-es **ehss**-beh-shtek
Is this made of wood/ paper/ metal/ copper/ pewter?	Ist dies aus Holz/ Papier/ Metall/ Kupfer/ Zinn?	ist dees ows holts/ pah-**peer**/meh-**tahl**/ **kup**-fehr/tsin
What kind of toys do you have?	Was für Spielzeuge haben Sie?	vahs fewr **shpeel**-tsoyg-eh **haab**-en zee
For a five-year-old boy/a five-year-old girl?	Für einen 5-jährigen Jungen/ein 5-jähriges Mädchen?	fewr **ine**-en fewnf-**yair**-ee-gehn **yung**-en/ine fewnf-**yair**-ee-gehs **mait**-khehn
For a ten-year-old child?	Für ein zehnjähriges Kind?	fewr ine **tsayn**-yay-ree-gehs kint
Do you have a/an	*Haben Sie ...*	**haab**-*en* zee
chess set	ein Schachspiel	ine **shakh**-shpeel
doll	eine Puppe	**ine**-eh **pup**-peh
electronic game	ein elektronisches Spiel	ine ayl-ek-**troan**-ish-ehs shpeel

PORCELAIN AND FINE ART

Meißner Porzellan in Dresden has been world famous for years and many firms such as Rosenthal and Tischenreuter are held in high esteem. Some early porcelain pieces are very expensive and can be found in antique shops. The modern Hummel figures enjoy great popularity. While Berlin's **Flohmarkt U-Bahnhof Nollendorf Platz** (flea market of the Nollendorf Platz subway station) offers thousands of knick-knacks, Vienna's **Doretheum**, with branches throughout Austria, offers a great variety of assorted antiques, or sometimes even an auction. The English "bull in the china shop" becomes in German "**Der Elefant im Porzellanladen.**" You can buy bulls or elephants and entire menageries in glass or porcelain everywhere in a German-speaking country in Europe.

I am interested in...	*Ich interessiere mich für...*	*ikh in-teh-reh-seer-eh mikh fewr*
Hummel figures	Hummelfiguren	**hum**-el-fi-goor-en
woodcarvings by Riemenschneider and Stoss	Holzschnitzereien von Riemenschneider und Stoss.	**holts**-shnits-eh-reye-en fon **reeem**-en-shneyed-er unt Stoss
classical/ medieval/ modern art	antike/ mittelalterliche/ moderne Kunst	ahn-**teek**-eh/**mit**-el-ahl-tehr-likh-eh/moh-**dehrn**-eh kunst
engravings by Dürer	Stiche von Dürer	**shtikh**-eh fon **dewr**-er
paintings by Holbein	Gemälde von Holbein	geh-**mayld**-eh fon **hol**-bine
handcarved crucifixes	handgeschnitzte Kruzifixe	**hahnt**-geh-shnitst-eh kru-tsee-**fiks**-eh
Russian icons	russische Ikonen	**ru**-ssi-sheh ee-**kohn**-en
Do you have something smaller/ bigger/ cheaper/older?	Haben Sie etwas Kleineres/ Größeres/ Billigeres/ Älteres?	**haab**-en zee **eht**-vahs **kline**-eh-res/**grers**-seh-res/**bil**-ig-eh-res **ehlt**-eh-res
That's too much to carry.	Das ist zu viel zu tragen.	dahs ist tsoo feel tsoo **traag**-en
I just want a small souvenir.	Ich möchte nur ein kleines Andenken.	ikh **merkht**-eh noor ine **kline**-es **ahn**-dehnk-en
What are the shipping charges to Canada?	Was sind die Versand-kosten nach Kanada?	Vahs zint dee fehr-**zahnt**-kost-en nakh **kah**-nah-dah
I don't want any trouble at customs.	Ich will keine Schwierig-keiten beim Zoll haben.	ikh vil **kine**-eh **shvee**-rikh-kite-en bime tsol **haab**-en

BOOKS, NEWSPAPERS, MAGAZINES AND STATIONERY

In Germany, bookshops and stationers' are usually separate shops, although the latter will often sell paperbacks, too. Larger bookstores usually stock English-language and other foreign-language publications. Newspapers, magazines and postcards are almost always available at a newsstand.

Shopper:	Where can I find English-language newspapers/magazines/books?
(Kundin):	Wo finde ich englisch-sprachige Zeitungen/Zeitschriften/Bücher?
	(voh **fin**-deh ikh **ehng**-lish shprahkh-ee-geh **tsite**-ung-en/**tsite**-shrif-ten)
Salesperson:	Please follow me. Here they are.
(Verkäufer):	Bitte folgen Sie mir. Hier sind sie.
	(**bit**-eh **fol**-gehn zee meer. here zint zee.)

Where is the nearest...?	*Wo ist der/die/das nächste...?*	*voh ist dehr/dee/dahs naikh-steh*
bookshop	Buchhandlung	**bookh**-hanhd-lung
newsstand	Zeitungsstand	**tsite**-ungs-shtant
stationer's	Schreibwarengeschäft	**shripe**-vah-rehn-geh-shehft

Where can I find a...?	*Wo finde ich...?*	*voh fin-deh ikh*
ballpoint pen	einen Kugelschreiber	**ine**-en **koo**-gel-shry-ber
calendar	einen Kalender	**ine**-en kah-**lehn**-der
crayons	Buntstifte	**bunt**-shtif-teh
envelopes	Briefumschläge	**breef**-oom-shlay-geh
eraser	einen Radiergummi	**ine**-en rah-**deer**-goom-ee
felt-tip pen	einen Filzstift	**ine**-en **filts**-shtift
guide book	einen Reiseführer	**ine**-en **ry**-zeh-few-rehr
map of the town	einen Stadtplan	**ine**-en **shtat**-plaan
notebook	ein Notizheft	ine no-**teets**-hehft
paperclips	Büroklammern	bew-**roh**-klahm-mern
pencil	einen Bleistift	**ine**-en **blye**-shtift
pencil sharpener	einen Bleistiftspitzer	**ine**-en **blye**-shtift-shpit-ser
pocket calculator	einen Taschenrechner	**ine**-en **tahsh**-en-rehkh-ner
postcards	Postkarten	**post**-kahr-tehn

Where can I find a...?	Wo finde ich...?	voh fin-**deh** ikh
road map of...	eine Straßenkarte von...	ine-eh **straa**-ssehn-kahr-teh fon
Scotch tape	Tesafilm	**tay**-zah-film
stapler	eine Drahtheftmaschine	ine-eh **draht**-heft-mah shee-neh
staples	Heftklammern	**hehft**-klahm-mern
string	Schnur	shnoor
thumb tacks	Reißzwecken	**rice**-tsveh-ken
writing pad	einen Schreibblock	ine-en **shripe**-blok

CASSETTES, CDS AND VIDEOS

Do you have any CDs by...?	Haben Sie Compact Discs von...?	**haa**-ben zee compact discs fon
May I listen to this CD?	Darf ich diesen Compact Disc hören?	dahrf ikh **dee**-zen compact disc **hewr**-en

Where is the section of...?	Wo finde ich...?	voh fin-**deh** ikh
audiocassettes	Kassetten	kah-**seht**-ten
videocassettes	Videokassetten	**vee**-deh-oh-kah-**seht**-ten
chamber music	Kammermusik	**kahm**-mehr-moo-zeek
classical music	klassische Musik	**klahs**-sish-eh moo-zeek
folk music/folk songs	Volkmusik/Volkslieder	**folk**-moo-zeek/**folks**-lee-der
jazz	Jazz	jazz
pop music/hits	Popmusik/Schlager	**pop**-moo-zeek/**shlah**-ger
instrumental music	Instrumentalmusik	in-stru-mehn-**taal**-moo zeek
light music	Unterhaltungsmusik	un-tehr-**hahl**-tungs-moo-zeek
orchestral music	Orchestermusik	or-**keh**-stehr-moo-zeek

TOILETRIES

Here is a list of items that can be found in a **Drogerie** (drug store) or department store. For prescriptions and drugs, you need an **Apotheke** (pharmacy).

I'm looking for...	Ich suche...	ikh zookh-eh
I'd like a/an/some...	Ich hätte gern	ikh heht-teh gehrn...
	ein/eine...	ine/ine-eh
hairbrush	Haarbürste	haar-bewrst-eh
comb	Kamm	kahm
hairspray	Haarspray	haar-shpray
cleansing cream	Reinigungscreme	rine-ee-ungs-kraym
after-shave lotion	Rasierwasser	rah-zeer-vahs-ser
dental floss	Zahnseide	tsaan-zyed-eh
bubble bath	Schaumbad	shouwm-baat
condoms	Kondom	kon-doh-meh
deodorant	Desdodorant	deh-zoh-doh-rahnt
emery board	Nagelfeile	naa-gel-pfye-leh
nail clippers	Nagelzange	naa-gel-tsahng-eh
nail scissors	Nagelschehre	naa-gel-shayr-eh
nail polish	Nagellack	naa-gel-lahk
nail polish remover	Nagellackentferner	naa-gel-lahk-ehnt-fehrn-er
eye liner	Lidstift	leed-shtift
eye shadow	Lidschatten	leed-shaht-en
eye pencil	Augenbrauenstift	owg-en-brow-en-shtift
razor	Rasierapparat	rah-zeer-ah-pah-raat
razor blades	Rasierklingen	rah-zeer-kling-en
shaving creme	Rasiercreme	rah-zeer-kraym
shaving lotion	Rasierwasser	rah-zeer-vahs-er
shampoo	Haarwaschmittel	haar-vash-mit-el
foot powder	Fußpuder	foos-pood-er
lipstick	Lippenstift	lip-en-shtift
lipsalve	Lippenpomade	lip-en-poh-maa-deh
moisturizing cream	Feuchtigkeitscreme	foykh-tikh-kites-kraym
mascara	Wimperntusche	vimp-ehrn-tush-eh
mirror	Spiegel	shpeeg-el
mouthwash	Mundwasser	munt-vahs-er
sanitary napkins	Damenbinden	daam-en-bind-en
(disposable) diapers	(wegwerfbare)Windeln	(vehk-vehrf-baar-eh)
		vind-eln
face powder	Gesichtspuder	geh-zikhts-poo-der
perfume	Parfüm	pahr-fewm

I'm looking for...	Ich suche...	ikh zookh-eh
I'd like a/an/some...	Ich hätte gern	ikh heht-teh gehrn...
	ein/eine...	ine/ine-eh
rouge	Rouge/Schminke	roozh/**shmin**-keh
safety pins	Sicherheitsnadeln	**zikh**-er hites-**naa**-deln
soap	Seife	zye-feh
sponge	Schwamm	shvahm
suntan lotion	Sonnencreme/öl	**zon**-en-kraym/erl
talcum powder	Talkumpuder	**taal**-kum-poo-der
tampons	Tampons	**tahm**-pons
tissues	Papiertücher	pah-**peer**-tew-kher
toilet paper	Toilettenpapier	toi-**leht**-ten-pah-peer
toothbrush	Zahnbürste	**tsaan**-bewr-steh
toothpaste	Zahnpasta	**tsaan**-pahs-tah
towels	Handtücher	**hahnt**-tew-kher
tweezers	Pinzette	pin-**tseht**-eh

FOOD SHOPPING

In Germany, Austria and Switzerland food shopping is done in big grocery stores (**Lebensmittelgeschäft**) as well as in small neighborhood and specialty stores such as the butcher (**Schlächter**) or bakery shop (**Bäckerei**). The standard unit of weight for purchasing produce, cheese or any other food is the kilogram (**Kilo**); fractions thereof are 1000 grams, etc. (**tow**-zehnt **Gramm**, etc.). A pound is a little less than half a kilo or 450 grams. It would be a good idea to bring your own shopping bag since not all stores provide them or they make you pay for each one.

At the food store

Salesperson:	May I help you?
(Verkäufer):	Darf ich Ihnen helfen? (dahrf ikh **een**-en **hehlf**-en)
Shopper:	I'd like some cheese.
(Kundin):	Ich hätte gern etwas Käse.
	(ikh **heht**-teh gehrn **eht**-vahs **kay**-seh)
Salesperson:	How about this one here?
	Wie wäre es mit diesem hier?
	(vee **vehr**-eh ehs mit **deez**-em heer)

Shopper:	May I have a tasting sample?	
	Darf ich eine Kostprobe haben?	
	(dahrf ikh **ine**-eh **kost**-proh-beh **haab**-en)	
Salesperson:	Here we are. – And how is it?	
	Ja, bitte. – Und wie schmeckt er?	
	(yah, **bit**-eh. – unt vee shmeckt ehr)	
Shopper:	Terrific. I'll take half a pound.	
	Wunderbar. Ich nehme ein halbes Pfund.	
	(**voon**-dehr-bahr. ikh **nehm**-eh ine **hahlb**-es pfunt)	

What sort of cheese do you have?	Welche Käsesorten haben Sie?	**vehl**-kheh **kay**-zeh-zor-tehn **haab**-en zee
I'd like some bread, please.	Ich möchte ein Brot, bitte.	ikh **merkht**-eh ine broht **bit**-teh

A piece of ...	*Ein Stück...*	*ine shtewk*
this one	von diesem	fon **deez**-em
the one on the shelf	von dem auf dem Regal	fon dehm owf dehm reh-**gaal**

I'll have one of those, please.	Ich möchte eins von denen, bitte.	ikh **murkh**-teh ines fon **dehn**-en **bit**-teh
May I help myself?	Kann ich mich selbst bedienen?	kahn ikh mikh zehlpst beh-**deen**-en

Please give me...	*Geben Sie mir, bitte...*	*gay-ben zee meer, bit-teh*
a kilo of apples	ein Kilo Äpfel	ine **kee**-loh **ehpf**-el
half a kilo of tomatoes	ein halbes Kilo Tomaten	ine **hahl**-behs **kee**-loh to-**maht**-en
a pound of butter	ein Pfund Butter	ine pfunt **but**-ter

Please give me...	*Geben Sie mir, bitte...*	*gay-ben zee meer, bit-teh*
300 grams of salami	Dreihundert Gramm Salami	dry-hun-dert grahm zah-**lah**-me
four slices of ham	vier Scheiben Schinken	feer **shib**-en **shink**-en
a bottle of juice	eine Flasche Saft	**ine**-eh **flahsh**-eh zahft
half a dozen eggs	ein halbes Dutzend Eier	ine **hahl**-behs **dut**-sehnt **eye**-yer

Please give me...	*Geben Sie mir, bitte...*	gay-*ben zee meer, bit-teh*
a box of cereal	ein Karton Müsli	ine kahr-**tong mews**-lee
a liter of milk	einen Liter Milch	**ine**-en **leet**-er milkh
a can of tomato sauce	eine Dose Tomatensauce	**ine**-eh **dohz**-eh toh-**maat**-en-zohss-eh
a package of	eine Packung	ine-eh **pahk**-ung
coffee/tea	Kaffee/Tee	**kah**-feh/teh
a jar of jam	ein Glas Marmelade	ine glaas mahr-meh-**laa**-deh
a can of beans	eine Dose Bohnen	**ine**-eh **dohz**-eh **boh**-nen
a cup of yogurt	einen Becher Yogurt	ine-en **behkh**-er **yo**-gurt
a package of candies	ein Paket Bonbons	ine pah-**keht** bohng-**bohngs**
a box of chocolates	eine Schachtel Schokolade	**ine**-eh **shakht**-el shok-oh-**laad**-eh
a tube of mustard	eine Tube Senf	**ine**-eh **too**-beh zehnf

Ketchup is not used as readily or as liberally as it is in North America. You are more likely to find mustard on every table and you'll have to ask for the ketchup!

CHAPTER SEVEN

Meeting and socializing

As in any country, meeting people is one of the best ways to find out more about a new culture and improve your language skills. Europeans are generally a little more reserved than North Americans but a genuine interest in your host country and a little patience and perseverance will usually overcome most barriers.

When meeting or saying goodbye, German speakers will usually shake hands; close friends will embrace. Unlike the French, Germans do *not* exchange kisses.

The introduction

Liz Jones:	Hello, may I introduce myself? My name is Liz Jones.
	Guten Tag, darf ich mich vorstellen? Ich heiße Liz Jones.
	(**goo**-ten tahk, dahrf ikh mikh **for**-shteh-len? ikh **hice**-seh liz jones)
Jürgen Graf:	Pleased to meet you. My name is Jürgen Graf. Are you here on business?
	Ich freue mich Sie kennenzulernen. Ich heiße Jürgen Graf. Sind Sie hier geschäftlich?
	(ikh **froy**-eh mikh zee **kehn**-nen-tsoo-lehr-nen. ikh **hice**-seh **yewr**-gen graaf. zint zee heer geh-**shehft**-likh)
Liz:	Yes, I'm staying two more weeks.
	Ja, ich bleibe noch zwei Wochen.
	(yaa, ikh **blye**-beh nokh tsvy **vokh**-en)

43

Jürgen:	Great. Perhaps we could see each other again.
	Super. Vielleicht könnten wir uns noch einmal sehen.
	(zoo-pehr. fel-**likht kurn**-ten veer uhns nokh ine-maal **zay**-en)
Liz:	That would be nice. How about Monday at 8 p.m. at the...theatre?
	Das wäre nett. Wie wäre es mit Montag um 20 Uhr am...Kino?
	(dahs **vay**-reh neht. vee **vay**-reh ehs mit **moon**-taak oom **tsvaan**-tseek oor um **kee**-noh)
Jürgen:	Wunderbar. See you then.
	Wunderbar. Bis dann. (**voon**-dehr-bahr. bis dahn)

GREETINGS AND INTRODUCTIONS

What's your name?	Wie heißen Sie?	Vee **hice**-en zee
My name is...	Ich heiße...	ikh **hice**-eh...
I'd like to introduce myself.	Ich möchte mich vorstellen.	ikh **murkh**-teh mikh **for**-shtehl-len
I'd like to introduce you to	Ich möchte Ihnen... vorstellen.	ikh murkh-teh **ee**-nen... **for**-shtehl-len
May I introduce... ?	*Darf ich... vorstellen?*	*dahrf ikh...for-shtehl-en*
my wife	meine Frau	**mine**-eh frow
my husband	meinen Mann	mine-nen mahn
my son	meinen Sohn	**mine**-nen zohn
my colleague	meinen Kollegen/ meine Kollegin	**mine**-en ko-**lay**-gehn/ **mine**-eh ko-**lay**-gin
my friend	meinen Freund/ meine Freundin	**mine**-nen froynt/ **mine**-neh **froyn**-din
Pleased to meet you.	Nett, Sie kennenzulernen.	neht, zee **kehn**-nen-tsoo-lehr-nen
How are you?	Wie geht es Ihnen?	vee gayt ehs **ee**-nen
Fine thanks, and you?	Danke gut. Und Ihnen?	**dahn**-keh goot unt **ee**-nen
How are you?	Wie geht's?*	vee gayt's

44

> **Wie geht's** is used informally between friends, relatives and children. For hotel people and people you meet on the train, be formal: **Wie geht es Ihnen?**

First meeting

English	German	Pronunciation
Are you German/Swiss/Austrian?	Sind Sie aus Deutschland/ der Schweiz/Österreich?	zint zee ows **doych**-lahnt/dehr shvites/ **ur**-steh-ryekh
Where are you from?	Woher kommen Sie?	voh-**hehr kom**-men zee
I'm from Canada.	Ich bin aus Kanada.	ikh bin ows **kah**-nah-dah
Where do you live?	Wo wohnen Sie?	voh **voh**-nen zee
I live in Toronto.	Ich wohne in Toronto.	ikh **voh**-neh in tor-on-toh
How long have you been here?	Wie lange sind Sie schon hier?	vee **lahng**-eh zint zee shohn heer
We've been here a week.	Wir sind schon seit einer Woche hier.	veer zint shohn zite **ine**-er **vokh**-eh heer

How do you like...?	*Wie gefällt Ihnen ...?*	*vee geh*-fehlt ee-*nen*
Germany	Deutschland?	**doych**-lahnt
Switzerland	die Schweiz?	dee schvites
Austria	Österreich?	**ur**-steh-ryekh

I don't know yet	Ich weiß noch nicht.	ikh vice nohkh nikht
I just arrived.	Ich bin gerade angekommen.	ikh bin geh-**raa**-deh **ahn**-geh-kom-men
I like it a lot here.	Mir gefällt es hier sehr gut.	meer geh-**fehlt** ehs heer zehr goot

Everything is so...	*Alles is so...*	*ah-les ist zoh*
interesting	interessant	in-teh-rehs-**sahnt**
different	anders	**ahn**-dehrs
beautiful	schön	shurn

There are two forms of address in German: the formal **Sie** and the informal **du** (both meaning *you*). Younger people will tend to be more willing to use the informal address right away, especially with people their own age, and adults address children under the age of 16 (approximately) as **du**. Otherwise, the guidelines for switching from the formal to the informal are sometimes a little vague and may change from region to region. It is best to be on the safe side and stick to the formal **Sie** until the native speaker invites the switch (**Warum duzen wir uns nicht?** – Why don't we use the **du** form with each other?).

MAKING FRIENDS

May I invite you ...?	*Darf ich Sie... einladen?*	*dahrf ikh zee ine-laa-den*
for a cup of tea	zu einer Tasse Tee	tsoo **ine**-er **tahs**-eh tay
for a glass of wine	zu einem Glas Wein	tsoo **ine**-em glaas vine
to lunch/dinner	zum Mittagessen/ Abendessen	tsoom **mit**-taak ehs-sen/ **aa**-behnt-ehs-sen
Can I get you a drink?	Möchten Sie etwas trinken?	**murkh**-ten zee **eht**-vahs **trin**-ken
With pleasure, thanks.	Mit Vergnügen, danke.	mit fehrk-**gnew**-gen, **dahn**-keh
Are you married?	Sind Sie verheiratet?	zint zee fehr-**hye**-raa-tet
No, I'm ...	*Nein, ich bin ...*	*nine, ikh bin*
single	ledig	**leh**-dikh
divorced	geschieden	geh-**shee**-den
a widow(er)	Witwe/Witwer	**vit**-veh/**vit**-ver
Are you travelling alone?	Reisen Sie allein?	rye-zen zee ah-**line**
I'm here with friends.	Ich bin mit Feunden hier.	ikh bin mit **froyn**-den heer

My family is travelling with me.	Meine Familie reist auch mit.	mine-eh fam-meel-yeh reyst awkh mit
Are you free this evening/tomorrow?	Sind Sie heute abend/morgen frei?	zint zee hoy-teh aa-behnt/mor-gen frye
May I telephone you?	Darf ich Sie anrufen?	dahrf ikh zee anh-roo-fen
What is your phone number?	Wie ist Ihre Telefonnummer?	vee ist ee-reh tay-lay-fohn-num-mer?
What is your address?	Wie ist Ihre Adresse?	vee ist ee-reh ah-drehs-seh

Would you like to go with us...?	*Möchten Sie mit uns... gehen?*	murkh-*ten zee mit uns...*gay-*en?*
to the movies	ins Kino	ins kee-noh
to a party	zu einer Party	tsoo ine-er paar-tee

Great, I'd love to come.	Prima. Ich komme sehr gerne mit.	pree-mah, ikh kom-meh zehr gehr-neh mit
Where shall we meet?	Wo treffen wir uns?	voh trehf-fen veer uns
It's getting late.	Es wird spät.	ehs virt shpayt
Thanks for everything.	Vielen Dank für alles.	fee-len dahnk fewr ah-les

DECLINING INVITATIONS

Sometimes you may not be interested in making friends or you may want to be left alone.

I am really very busy.	Ich habe keine Zeit.	ikh haa-beh kine-eh tsite
Thank you, perhaps another time.	Danke, vielleicht ein anderes Mal.	dahn-keh feel-likht ine ahn-deh-rehs maal
I am married.	Ich bin verheiratet.	ikh bin fehr-hi-raa-teht
My husband/boyfriend will be right back.	Mein Mann/Freund wird gleich zurück sein.	mine mahn/froynd virt glykh tsoo-rewk sine
My wife/girlfriend will be right back.	Meine Frau/Freundin wird gleich zurück sein.	mine-neh frow/froyn-din virt glykh tsoo-rewk sine

When invited to a home for dinner, flowers are an appropriate gesture. Wine is also a nice gift, but flowers are preferable.

English	German	Pronunciation
You are boring.	Sie sind mir zu langweilig.	zee zint meer tsoo **lahng**-vile-likh
I am not interested in you.	Ich bin nicht an Ihen interessiert.	ikh bin nikht ahn ee-nen in-teh-rehs-**seert**
Leave me alone.	Lassen Sie mich in Ruhe.	**lah**-sehn zee mikh in roo-heh
I have had enough.	Jetzt reicht es mir.	yehtst rykht ehs meer
Get lost, otherwise I will call the police.	Verschwinden Sie, sonst rufe ich die Polizei.	fehr-**shvin**-dehn zee, sonst **roo**-feh ikh dee poh-lee-**tsye**

THE FAMILY

English	German	Pronunciation
I have...	Ich habe	ikh haa-beh
a large/small family	eine große/kleine Familie	ine-eh **grohs**-seh/**kline**-eh fah-**meel**-yeh
a husband/a wife	einen Mann/eine Frau	ine-en mahn/ine-eh frow
two children	zwei Kinder	tsvye **kin**-der
a daughter/two daughters	eine Tochter/zwei Töchter	ine-eh **tohkh**-teh/tsvye **turkh**-ter
a son/two sons	einen Sohn/zwei Söhne	ine-en zohn/tsvye **zur**-neh
a baby	ein Baby	ine **bay**-bee
a brother/two brothers	einen Bruder/zwei Brüder	ine-en **broo**-der/tsvye **brew**-der
a sister/two sisters	eine Schwester/zwei Schwestern	ine-eh **shvehs**-ter/tsvye **shvehs**-tern
a mother/father/ parents	eine Mutter/einen Vater/Eltern	ine-eh **mut**-ter/**ine**-en **faa**-ter/**ehl**-tern
How old are your children?	Wie alt sind Ihre Kinder?	vee aalt zint **ee**-reh **kin**-der
Peter is five years old.	Peter ist fünf Jahre alt.	**pay**-ter is fewnf **yaa**-reh aalt
He is younger/older than Paul.	Er ist jünger/älter als Paul.	ehr ist **yewn**-ger/**ehl**-ter ahls powl

Driving a car

CAR RENTALS

Most major car rental agencies have branches in German-speaking countries, but it is easier and more economical to rent a car before you arrive. If you don't drive a car with a stick shift, make sure you request a car with an automatic transmission. You can use your Canadian driver's license to drive and rent a car but if you are renting for more than a month, you may need an international driver's license (available at your local branch of the Canadian Automobile Association.)

The legal driving age is 18, but some car rental companies have set higher limits. Many car rental companies allow you to pick up and drop off cars at offices throughout Germany, but check with individual agencies about this.

It's always a good idea to pick up a listing of current international road signs and symbols at the CAA before you leave on your trip.

You can sometimes arrange deals in Canada to buy a German car, travel with it and then have your car shipped home or sold in Europe after your vacation.

At the car rental agency

Traveller:	I would like to rent a car.
(Reisender):	Ich möchte einen Wagen mieten.
	(ikh **murkh**-teh ine-en **vah**-gen **mee**-ten)
Employee:	We can offer you a VW Passat with automatic.
(Angestellte):	Wir können Ihnen einen VW Passat mit Automatik anbieten.
	(veer **kur**-nen **ee**-nen ine-en fow vah mit ow-toh-mah-tik **ahn**-bee-ten)
Traveller:	I'd just like to have it for the weekend.
	Kann ich ihn nur über das Wochenende haben.
	(kahn ikh een noor **ew**-ber dahs **vohkh**-en-en-deh **haa**-ben)
Employee:	Of course. That way you get a special price, including unlimited mileage.
	Sicher, so bekommen Sie einen Sonderpreis, inklusive unbegrenzter Kilometerzahl.
	(**zikh**-er, zoh beh-**kom**-men zee ine-en **zon**-dehr-price, in-klu-**zee**-veh un-beh-**grehnts**-ter kee-loh-**may**-ter-tsaal)
Traveller:	Great.
	Wunderbar. (**vun**-dehr-baar)
Employee:	May I see your driver's license?
	Darf ich Ihren Führerschein sehen?
	(dahrf ikh **ee**-ren **few**-rer-shine **zah**-en)

Is there a car rental office nearby?	Gibt es eine Autovermietung in der Nähe?	gihpt es ine-eh **ow**-toh-fehr-mee-tung in dehr **nay**-eh
I like to rent (a) ...	*Ich möchte... mieten.*	*ikh* murkh-*teh* mee-*ten*
small/subcompact car.	einen Kleinwagen	ine-en **kline**-vaa-gen
midsize car	einen Mittelklassewagen	ine-en **mit**-tel-klah-se-vaa-gen
large car	einen großen Wagen	ine-en **grohs**-en vaa-gen
station wagon	einen Kombiwagen	ine-en **kom**-bee-vaa-gen
convertible	ein Kabriolett	ine kah-bree-oh-**lay**

I like to rent (a) ...	*Ich möchte...*	***ikh** murkh-teh*
	mieten.	mee-*ten*
car with automatic	einen Wagen mit	ine-en **vaa**-gen mit ow-
transmission.	Automatic	toh-**mah**-tic
your least expensive car	Ihren preiswertesten	ee-ren **price**-vehr-tehs-
	Wagen	ten **vaa**-gen
How much does it cost	*Wieviel kosten es*	vee-*feel* kohs-*tet es*
per...?	*pro ...?*	*proh*
day/week/month/	Tag/Woche/Monat/	tahk/**vokh**-eh/**moh**-naat/
kilometre	Kilometer	**kee**-loh-may-ter
I'd like a comprehensive	Ich möchte eine Voll-	ikh **murkh**-teh ine-eh -
insurance.	kaskoversicherung.	**fol**-kahs-koh-fehr-**sikh**-
		eh-rung
Does the rental price	Ist unbegrenzte	ist un-beh-**grehns**-teh
include unlimited	Kilometer-zahl im	**kee**-loh-may-ter-tsahl im
mileage?	Mietpreis inbe-griffen?	**meet**-price **in**-beh-grif-en
I want to rent the car here	Ich will das Auto hier	ikh vill dahs **ow**-toh heer
and leave it in Berlin.	mieten und es in Berlin	**mee**-en unt in behr-**leen**
	wieder abgeben.	wee-dehr **ahp**-gay-ben
Can I leave the car	Kann ich den Wagen	kahn ikh dehn **vaa**-gen
in another city?	anderswo zurückgeben?	**ahn**-dehrs-voh tsoo--
		rewk gay-ben
Is there an additional	Entstehen mir dadurch	ehnt-**shtay**-en meer daa-
charge for that?	zusätzliche Kosten?	**durkh tsoo**-zehts-likh-eh
		kost-en
Here is my driver's	Hier haben Sie meinen	heer **haa**-ben zee **mine**-
license.	Führerschein.	en **fewr**-ehr-shine
Do you need my	Brauchen Sie meine	**brow**-khen zee **mine**-eh
credit card?	Kreditkarte?	krah-**deet**-kahr-teh
Do you have a road map/	Haben Sie eine Landkarte/	**haa**-ben zee ine-eh **lahnt**
of the city?	einen Stadtplan?	kehr-teh/**ine**-en **shtaht**-
		plahn

ON THE ROAD

In general, Germany, Austria and Switzerland have extensive and well-maintained highway networks and roads. Even the roads of the former East German provinces (**Länder**) have been brought up to meet the quality of highway travel in Europe. Highways (**Autobahn**) are free in Germany, although there is a good chance of some form of toll in the future. To use the superhighway in Switzerland, you must purchase a Vignette (sticker) for your windshield, which is available as you cross the border. In Austria, some tunnels charge tolls (**die Maut**).

The recommended speed in Germany is 130 kilometres (80 miles) per hour. However, the speed of some drivers will take your breath away. Make sure not to stay in the passing lane except when passing another vehicle. If you have the luxury of time, you may prefer to plan your route along the more scenic secondary highways, particularly the well-known roads along vineyards (**Weinstraßen**) and romantic roads (**Romantische Straßen**). Always try to avoid rush hour in and around the cities and the seasonal peak traffic periods during school holidays. You may also want to inquire about road works in the country. You can get information on road and traffic conditions by radio, which interrupt their programming to give you the latest updates on accidents (**Unfälle**) and traffic jams (**Stau**).

Besides parking lots and meters, larger towns and cities also have Blue Zones where you need a parking disk (**Parkscheibe**), available at no cost from tourist offices, gas stations, automobile clubs and hotels. This honor-system parking option requires you to set your arrival time on the disk, display it on your windshield and then leave within the allotted time.

A red reflector warning triangle must be carried for use in case of a breakdown, and seat belts (**Sicherheitsgurt**) are obligatory.

Asking directions

Pardon me...	Entschuldigen Sie, bitte...	ehnt-**shul**-dee-gen zee, **bit**-eh
Is this the road to ...?	Ist dies die Straße nach ...?	ist dees dee **shtrah**-seh nahkh
Where does the road lead?	Wohin führt diese Straße?	**voh**-hin fewrt **dee**-zeh **shtrah**-seh
I have lost my way.	Ich habe mich verfahren.	ikh **haa**-beh mikh vehr-**faa**-ren
I got lost because of the detour.	Wegen der Umleitung habe ich mich verfahren.	**vay**-gen dehr **um**-light-ung **haa**-beh ikh mikh fehr-**faa**-ren
Can you tell me how to get to...	Können Sie mir sagen wie ich nach ... komme?	**kur**-nen zee meer **zah**-gen, vee ikh nahkh... **kom**-meh
Am I on the right road now?	Bin ich jetzt auf der richtigen Straße?	bin ikh yetst owf dehr **rikh**-tee-gen **straa**-seh
How far is it to the next city?	Wie weit ist es zur nächsten Stadt?	vee vite ist ehs bis tsoor **naykh**-sten shtaht
What's the next town called?	Wie heißt die nächste Ort?	vee heyst dehr **naykhs**-teh ort
Can you show it to me on the map?	Können Sie es mir auf der Landkarte zeigen?	**kern**-en zee es meer owf dehr **lahnt**-kahr-teh **tsey**-gen
Is there a better/faster/ less congested road?	Gibt es eine bessere/ schnellere/weniger befahrene Straße?	gibt es **ine**-eh **behs**-seh-reh/**shnehl**-leh-reh/**vay**-nee-ger beh-**fah**-rehn-eh **shtrah**-seh
Should I drive straight ahead/to the left/right?	Soll ich geradeaus/links/ oder rechts fahren?	zol ikh geh-**raa**-deh-ows/links/oh-der rekhts **faa**-ren
At the next (second, third) traffic light?	Bei der nächsten (zweiten, dritten) Ampel?	bey dehr **naykhs**-ten (**tsvey**-ten, **drit**-ten) **ahm**-pel
Where should I turn?	Wo soll ich abbiegen?	voh zol ikh **ahp**-bee-gen
Are there road signs, or should I ask again there?	Ist es gut beschildert, oder soll ich dort wieder fragen?	ist es goot beh-**shil**-dehrt, **ohd**-dehr zol ikh dohrt vee-dehr **frah**-gen

Do not stop on the shoulder of the **Autobahn** unless it is an emergency. It is against the law and you may be fined. Rest areas are provided along the expressways for bathroom stops, drinks and a stretch.

What's the best road for me to take to get to the Autobahn?	Wie fahre ich am besten zur Autobahneinfahrt?	vee **faar**-eh ikh ahm **behst**-en tsoor **ow**-toh-baan-ine-fahrt
Highway exit	Ausfahrt	**ows**-fahrt
May I park here?	Darf ich hier parken?	dahrf ikh heer **pahr**-ken
Is there a parking lot near here?	Gibt es einen Parkplatz in der Nähe?	gipt ehs **ine**-en **pahrk**-plahts in der **nay**-heh
Do you have change for the parking meter?	Haben Sie Kleingeld für die Parkuhr?	**haa**-ben zee **kline**-gehlt fewr dee **pahrk**-oor

AT THE SERVICE STATION

I'm looking for a gas station.	Ich suche eine Tankstelle.	ikh **zookh**-eh **ine**-eh **tahnk**-stehl-eh
Where is the nearest gas station (with service/ with self service)?	Wo ist die nächste Tankstelle (mit Bedienung/ mit Selbstbedienung)?	voo ist dee **naykhs**-teh **tahnk**-shtehl-eh (mitbeh-dee-nung/mit **zehlpst**-beh-dee-nung)
Fill it up, please, with...	*Volltanken, bitte, mit...*	fol-*tahn-ken*, bit-*teh mit*
regular/super	Normal/Super.	nor-**mahl**/zoo-pehr
unleaded	mit bleifreiem Benzin.	mit **blye**-fry-em ben-**tseen**
diesel	Diesel.	**dee**-zel
Give me 40 litres of	*Geben Sie mir vierzig Liter*	gay-*ben zee meer* feer-*tsekh* **lee**-tehr
regular/super.	normal/super.	nor-**mahl**/**zoo**-pehr
Please check the...	*Prüfen Sie bitte...*	prew-*fen zee* bit-*teh*
oil	den Ölstand	dehn **url**-shtahnt
water	das Wasser	dahs **vahs**-er
battery	die Batterie	dee bah-teh-**ree**

54

Please check the...	*Prüfen Sie bitte...*	prew-*fen* zee bit-*teh*
brake fluid	die Bremsflüssigkeit	dee **brehms**-flews-sikh-kite
carburetor	den Vergaser	dehn fehr-**gaaz**-er
spark plugs	die Zündkerzen	dee **tsewnt**-kehrts-en
ignition system	die Zündung	dee **tsewnd**-ung
lights	die Beleuchtung	dee beh-**loykht**-ung
tire pressure	den Reifendruck	dehn **rey**-fen-drook
spare tire	den Ersatzreifen	dehn ehr-**zahts**-rye-fen
Please change the...	*Wechseln Sie bitte...*	vehk-*seln* zee bit-*teh*
the tire	den Reifen	dehn **rye**-fen
oil	das Motoröl	dahs moh-**tohr**-url
fan belt	den Keilriemen	dehn **kile**-ree-men
wipers	die Scheibenwischer	dee **shye**-ben-vish-er
spark plugs	die Zündkerzen	dee **tsewnt**-kehr-tsen
Please clean the windshield.	Reinigen Sie bitte die Windschutzscheibe.	**rye**-nee-gen zee **bit**-teh dee **vint**-shoots-shye-beh
Where are the toilets?	Wo sind die Toiletten?	voh zint dee toh-**let**-en

CAR PROBLEMS

Where is the nearest garage (for repairs)?	Wo ist die nächste Reparaturwerkstatt?	voh ist dee **naykh**-steh reh-pah-rah-**toor**-vehrk-staht
Can you send a mechanic?	Können Sie einen Mechaniker schicken?	**kur**-nen zee **ine**-nen meh-**khah**-ni-kehr **shik**-ken
Excuse me, my car has broken down.	Entschuldigung, mein Wagen hat eine Panne.	ehnt-**shool**-dee-gung, mine **vaa**-gen haht **ine**-eh **pahn**-eh
It won't start.	Er springt nicht an.	ehsr sprinkt nikht ahn
The battery is dead.	Die Batterie ist leer.	dee bah-teh-**ree** ist lehr
The engine is overheated.	Der Motor läuft zu heiß.	dehr moh-**tohr** loyft tsoo hice
The radiator is leaking.	Der Kühler ist undicht.	dehr **kewl**-ehr ist un-dikht
I have a flat tire.	Ich habe einen Platten.	ikh **haa**-beh **ine**-en **plaht**-en

I've run out of gas.	Der Tank ist leer.	dehr tahnk ist lehr
I've locked the keys in the car.	Ich habe die Schlüssel im Wagen eingeschlossen	ikh **haa**-beh dee **shlews**-sel **vaa**-gen **ine**-geh-shlos-sen
There is something wrong with the...	*... ist/sind nicht in Ordnung*	*... ist/zint nikht in ort-nung*
brakes	die Bremsen	dee **brehm**-zen
directional lights	die Blinklichter	dee **blink**-likh-ter
headlights	die Scheinwerfer	dee **shine**-vehr-fer
electrical system	die elektrische Anlage	dee eh-**lehk**-trish-eh **ahn**-lah-geh
starter	der Anlasser	dehr **ahn**-lahs-sehr
ignition	die Zündung	dee **tsyn**-dung
carburetor	der Vergaser	dehr vehr-**gah**-zehr
radiator	der Kühler	dehr **kew**-ler
transmission	das Getriebe	dahs geh-**tree**-beh
exhaust pipe	der Auspuff	dehr **ows**-puf
wheel	ein Rad	ine raht
Can you send a tow truck?	Können Sie einen Abschleppwagen schicken?	**kur**-nen zee **ine**-en **ahp**-shlep-vaa-gen **shik**-ken
Do you have the parts?	Haben Sie die Ersatzteile?	**haa**-ben zee dee ehr-**sahts**-tile-eh
Can you repair it temporarily?	Können Sie es provisorisch reparieren?	**kern**-en zee ehs proh-vi-**zoh**-rish ray-pah-**ree**-rehn
How long will it take?	Wie lange wird es dauern?	vee **lahng**-eh wirt es dow-ern
Couldn't it possibly be done today?	Geht's vielleicht doch noch heute?	gayt's fee-**likht** dokh nokh **hoy**-teh
How much will it cost?	Wieviel wird es kosten?	**vee**-feel wirt es **kos**-ten
Is everything okay now?	Ist jetzt alles in Ordnung?	ist yehtst **ah**-lehs in **ort**-nung
Can I have an itemized bill for my insurance?	Kann ich eine detaillierte Rechnung für meine Versicherung haben?	kahn ikh **ine**-eh deh-tah-**yeer**-teh **rehkh**-nung fewr **mine**-eh fehr-**zikh**-eh-rung **haa**-ben

Accidents - police

English	German	Pronunciation
Please call the police.	Rufen Sie bitte die Polizei.	roo-fehn zee bit-teh dee poh-lee-tsigh
There has been an accident. It's about three km from here.	Es ist ein Unfall passiert, ungefähr drei km. von hier.	ehs ist ine un-fahl pah-seert, un-geh-fehr dry kee-loh-meh-ter fohn heer
Where is the nearest telephone?	Wo ist das nächste Telefon?	voh ist dahs naykhs-teh teh-leh-fohn
Call a doctor/an ambulance quickly.	Rufen Sie schnell einen Arzt/einen Krankenwagen.	roo-fehn zee shnehl ine-en ahrts/ine-nen krahn-ken vah-gen
There are people injured.	Es hat Verletzte gegeben.	ehs hat fehr-lehts-teh geh-geh-ben
Here's my driver's license.	Hier ist mein Führerschein.	heer ist mine few-rehr-shine
What's your name and address?	Ihren Namen und Anschrift bitte.	ee-rehn nah-mehn unt ahnt-shrift, bit-teh
I'd like to see your car insurance.	Ich möchte Ihre Autoversicherung, sehen.	ikh murkh-teh ee-reh ow-toh-fehr-sikh-eh-rung seh-en

Emergency telephone numbers

Police	110	(Germany)
	133	(Austria)
	117	(Switzerland)
Fire	112	(Germany)
	122	(Austria)
	118	(Switzerland)

CHAPTER NINE

Sightseeing

Tourists travel in order to learn more about the culture, history and language of the country they are visiting. Of course, it's a good idea to do some research about the places you want to see in advance. Information is available in tourist offices and travel agencies in the countries you are visiting. There are also some excellent travelling guides in bookstores and kiosks to help you plan your itinerary.

Germany is situated in the heart of Europe. It has nine neighbours and is a bridge to the countries of Central and Eastern Europe. Germany consists of 16 states known as **Länder**: Baden – Württemberg (Stuttgart), Bavaria (Munich), Berlin, Brandenburg (Potsdam), Bremen, Hamburg, Hessen (Wiesbaden), Mecklenburg – Western Pommerania (Schwerin), Lower Saxony (Hanover), North Rhine – Westphalia, (Düsseldorf), Rhineland – Palatinate (Mainz), Saarland (Saarbrücken), Saxony (Dresden), Saxony – Anhalt (Magdeburg), Schleswig – Holstein (Kiel), and Thuringia (Erfurt).

The climate in Germany is temperate and sharp changes in temperature are rare. There is precipitation all year round. In winter, the average temperature is between 5°C in the lowland areas and -6°C in the mountains. In the warmest month of the year, July, temperatures are between 18°C in low-lying regions and 20°C in the sheltered valleys of the south. The mountains have a climatic zone of their own with cold winds, cool summers and heavy snow in winter.

Apart from commercial travel operators, there is the German Tourist Board (DZT) which seeks to promote tourist travel to Germany. It publishes a wide range of brochures about the

Federal Republic in many languages. To obtain information about travel in Germany, contact:

Deutsche Zentrale für Tourismus
(German Central Tourist Board)
Beethovenstrasse 69
60325 Frankfurt am Main

Deutscher Fremdenverkehrsverband
(Tourist Industry Association)
Bertha-von-Suttner-Platz 13
53111 Bonn

Germany has a remarkable variety of beautiful towns and landscapes in a comparatively small area. In the north, visitors are drawn by the coasts and islands and the sea climate. Tourists also flock to the lakeland areas in Holstein and Mecklenburg, to the Central Upland and the Alps for hiking or skiing, or to Lake Constance and the Bavarian lakes in the south for water sports. Those looking for romantic scenery choose the valleys of the Rhine, Main, Mosel, Neckar, Danube and the Elbe rivers.

There are nearly 100 tourist routes, such as the German Fairy-Tale Route, the Romanesque Route, the Romantic Route or the German Wine Route, which take visitors away from the major traffic arteries, opening up the country's traditional landscapes and providing access to a great variety of attractions in idyllic old towns and villages.

In Bavaria tourists are surrounded by the extravagance of baroque architecture. In the north they encounter the severity of brick gothic buildings. Visitors can expect hospitality and the famous **Gemütlichkeit**, a word that is difficult to translate but expresses the idea of warmth and friendliness, the "good feeling."

Cuisine and accommodation are of a high standard, ranging from inexpensive rooms on a farm or at a guest house to luxury holiday resorts and top-class international hotels. Contrary to the popular belief, German cuisine does not consist solely of knuckle of pork and sauerkraut. For the gourmet there are an increasing number of restaurants that compare favorably with their French or Italian rivals. German wines have an excellent reputation and the fact that Germans know a great deal about brewing beer hardly needs mentioning!

TRANSPORTATION – IN THE CITY

All larger cities such as Berlin, Hamburg, München, Vienna and Zürich have the following modes of public transportation:

Busse buses
U-Bahn subway (white U sign on blue background)
Strassenbahn streetcars
S-Bahn suburban commuter train of German Rail
(white S sign on green background)

ATTRACTIONS

Where is the tourist office?	Wo ist das Fremden-verkehrsbüro?	voh ist dahs **frehm**-den fehr-kehrs-bew-roh
What are the most important things to see?	Was sind die wichtigsten Sehenswürdigkeiten?	vahs zint dee **vikh**-tikh-sten **zay**-ens-vewr-dikh-kite-en
Is there a guided tour of the city?	Gibt es eine Stadt-rundfahrt?	gipt ehs **ine**-eh **shtaht**-runt-faart
At what time is the tour?	Um wieviel Uhr ist die Rundfahrt?	um **vee**-feel oor ist dee **ruhnt**-faart
Will they pick us up at the hotel?	Holt man uns im Hotel ab?	hohlt mahn uns im ho-**tel** ahp
How long does it last?	Wie lange dauert sie?	vee **lahng**-eh **dow**-ert zee
How much does it cost?	Was kostet sie?	vahs **kos**-tet zee
Do you have a map of the town?	Haben Sie einen Stadtplan?	**haa**-ben zee ine-en **shtaht**-plaan
Where is the...?	*Wo ist/wo sind...?*	*voh ist/voh zint*
abbey	die Abtei	dee ahp-**tye**
amusement park	der Vergnügungspark	dehr fehr-**gnew**-gungks-paark
aquarium	das Aquarium	dahs ah-**kvah**-ree-oom
art galleries	die Kunstgalerien	dee **kunst**-gah-leh-ree-en
botanical garden	der Botanische Garten	dehr bo-**taa**-nish-eh **gaar**-ten
castle	das Schloß/die Burg	dahs shlos/dee boork
cathedral	der Dom/die Kathedrale	dehr dohm/dee kaa-tay-**draa**-leh
church	die Kirche	dee **keer**-kheh

city center/downtown	die Stadtmitte/das Zentrum/die Innenstadt	dee **shtat**-mit-teh/dahs **tsehn**-trum/dee **in**-nen-shtaht
city hall	das Rathaus	dahs **raat**-hows
city walls/ramparts	die Stadtmauern	dee **shtaht**-mow-ern
concert hall	die Konzerthalle	dee kon-**tsehrt**-hahl-leh
exhibition center	die Ausstellungshalle	dee **ows**-shtehl-lungs-hahl-leh
fountain	der (Spring-) Brunnen	dehr (**shpring**-) **brun**-nen
gardens	die Gärten/Grünanlagen	dee **gehr**-ten/**grewn**-ahn-laa-gen
library	die Bibliothek	dee beeb-lee-oh-**tayk**
market	der Markt	dehr mahrkt
museum	das Museum	dahs moo-**zay**-um
old part of town	die Altstadt	dee **ahlt**-shtaht
open-air stage	die Freilichtbühne	dee **frye**-likht-bew-neh

Where is the...?	*Wo ist/wo sind...?*	*voh ist/voh zint*
opera house	das Opernhaus/die Oper	dahs **oh**-pehrn-hows/dee **oh**-per
palace	der Palast	dehr pah-**lahst**
park	der Park	dehr pahrk
river	der Fluß	dehr flus
ruins	die Ruinen	dee roo-**ee**-nen
shopping district	das Einkaufsviertel	dahs **ine**-kowfs-feer-tel
stadium	das Stadion	dahs **shtaa**-dee-ohn
theatre	das Theater	dahs tay-**aa**-ter
tower	der Turm	dehr toorm
university	die Universität	dee oo-nee-vehr-zi-**tayt**
zoo	der Zoo	dehr tsoh

How old is that building?	Wie alt is das Gebäude?	vee ahlt ist dahs geh-**boy**-deh
Who built it?	Wer hat es gebaut?	vehr haht ehs geh-**bowt**
What monument is that?	Was für ein Denkmal ist das?	vahs fewr ine **dehnk**-maal ist dahs
Where can I get souvenirs?	Wo kann man Andenken kaufen?	woh kahn mahn **anh**-dehn-ken **kow**-fen

Museums offer guided tours, some in English. In some churches or parts of churches, you must pay admission and have an official guide. But you can also go through most museums and churches on your own. For palaces and castles, however, a group tour with a guide is the general rule.

Can the castle (museum, monument) be visited without a guide?	Kann man das Schloß (Museum, Denkmal) ohne Führung besichtigen?	kahn mahn dahs shloss (moo-**zay**-um, **denk**-maal) **ohn**-eh **fewr**-ung beh-**zikht**-ee-gen
What time does it open (close)?	Um wieviel Uhr wird geöffnet (geschlossen)?	um **vee**-feel oor veert geh-**erf**-net (geh-**shloss**-en)
How much is the admission for...	*Was kostet der Eintritt für...*	*vahs kos-tet dehr ine-trit fewr*
an adult	einen Erwachsenen	**ine**-en ehr-**vahk**-seh-nen
a child	ein Kind	ine kint
a senior	einen Rentner	**ine**-en **rehnt**-ner
I want three tickets.	Ich möchte drei Eintrittskarten.	ikh **merkh**-teh dreye **ine**-trits-kaar-ten
How long must one wait?	Wie lange muß man warten?	vee **lahng**-eh muss mahn **vaart**-en
Is it all right to go in now?	Darf man jetzt rein?	dahrf mahn yetst rine
Is taking photographs allowed?	Darf man photographieren?	dahrf mahn foh-toh-grah-**feer**-en
I am interested in...	*Ich interessiere mich für...*	*ikh in-teh-rehs-seer-reh mikh fewr*
antiques	Antiquitäten	ahn-tik-vee-**tay**-ten
anthropology	Anthropologie	ahn-tro-po-lo-**gee**
archaeology	Archäologie	ahr-keh-o-lo-**gee**
classical art	klassische Kunst	**klahs**-ish-eh kunst
modern art	moderne Kunst	mo-**dehr**-neh kunst
impressionist art	impressionistische Kunst	im-prehs-yoh-**nis**-tish-eh kunst
natural history	Naturkunde	nah-**toor**-kun-deh

painting	Malerei	maa-leh-**rye**
sculpture	Bildhauerei	**bilt**-how-eh-rye
Who is the artist?	Wer ist der Künstler?	vehr ist dehr **kewnst**-lehr
Who painted that picture?	Wer hat das Bild gemalt?	vehr haht dahs bilt geh-**maalt**
When was it painted?	Wann wurde es gemalt?	vahn **voor**-deh ehs geh-**maalt**
I think it is beautiful.	Ich finde es schön.	ikh **fin**-deh ehs shurn

TRANSPORTATION – CROSS COUNTRY

In 1991 the Deutsche Bundesbahn (German Federal Railway) introduced its first high-speed services. The new ICE trains (intercity express) can travel up to 250 km/h. The new routes between Hanover, Würzburg, Mannheim, Stuttgart and Munich make the railways even more attractive, especially for business travellers. The aim is to offer an attractive alternative to air and car travel over distances of up to 500 km.

On nearly all of Germany's roads there is a graduated speed limit. On national highways, it is usually 100 km/h, in built-up areas 50 km/h, and in some residential areas only 30 km/h. Only some parts of the Autobahns have no speed limit.

Apart from the excellent Autobahns, there is also a dense network of national highways and local roads. Long-distance rail travel is provided by comfortable trains, all of which have a dining car, and most of the night trains also have a sleeping car. Those who wish can also reserve a seat on car-carrying trains. All through the year, the Federal Railway offers cheap city tours and other special deals for young people. A cheap "railcard" can be used on all routes for a whole year to obtain tickets at half price.

At the station

The main stations in some of the larger cities (Berlin and Munich, for instance) have computerized timetable machines. Otherwise look for posted timetables:

Abfahrt in yellow is for departures
Ankunft in white is for arrivals

63

Where is/are the...?	*Wo ist/sind...?*	*voh ist/zint*
train station	der Bahnhof	dehr **baan**-hohf
information	die Auskunft	dee **ows**-kuhnft
ticket window	der Fahrkartenschalter	dehr **faar**-kahr-ten-shahl-ter
booking/reservation office	die Platzreservierung	dee **plahts**-reh-zehr-vee-rung
baggage check	die Gepäckaufbewahrung	dee geh-**pehk**-owf-beh-vaa-rung
baggage lockers	die Schließfächer	dee **shlees**-feh-kher

Where is/are the...?	*Wo ist/sind...?*	*voh ist/zint*
lost and found	das Fundbüro	dahs **funt**-bew-roh
restrooms	die Toiletten	dee toy-**leh**-ten
waiting room	der Wartesaal	dehr **vahr**-teh-zaal
exit	der Ausgang	dehr **ows**-gahng
a telephone	ein Telefon	ine teh-leh-**fohn**
platform 5	Bahnsteig 5	**bahn**-shtike fewnf
track 3	Gleis 3	glice drye
newsstand	der Zeitungsstand	dehr **tsi**-tungs-stahnt
restaurant	das Restaurant	dahs **rehs**-toh-rahnt
currency-exchange	die Wechselstube	dee **vehk**-sehl-shtoo-beh

TICKETS, RESERVATIONS AND ENQUIRIES

Traveller:
(Reisender):

I'd like a ticket to Hamburg.
Ich möchte eine Fahrkarte nach Hamburg.
(ikh **murkh**-teh **ine**-eh **faar**-kahr-teh nahkh **hahm**-buhrk)

Employee:
(Angestellter):

First or second class?
Erster oder zweiter Klasse?
(**ehr**-ster **oh**-der **tsvi**-ter **klah**-seh)

Traveller:

Second class. Do you have student rates?
Haben Sie einen Studententarif?
(**haa**-ben zee **ine**-en shtu-**dehn**-ten-taa-reef)

Employee:

Yes. Would you like a one-way or a round trip ticket?
Ja. Möchten Sie einfach oder retour?
(yaa. **murkh**-ten zee **ine**-fahkh **oh**-dehr **reh**-toor)

Traveller:	One way. Non-smoker, please. How much is the ticket?
	Einfach. Nichtraucher, bitte. Wieviel kostet die Fahrkarte?
	(ine-fahkh. **nikht**-row-kher, **bit**-teh. **vee**-feel **kohs**-tet dee **faar**-kahr-teh)
Employee:	Your train leaves at...
	Ihr Zug fährt um... (eer tsook fehrt um)

I'd like...	*Ich möchte...*	*ikh* murkh-*teh*
a window seat	einen Fensterplatz	**ine**-en **fehn**-ster-plahts
a couchette/bunk	einen Platz im	**ine**-en plahts im
	Liegewagen	**lee**-geh-vaa-gen
two berths in the	zwei Plätze im	tsvy **pleh**-tseh im
sleeping car	Schlafwagen	**shlaaf**-vaa-gen
to check the bags	dieses Gepäck aufgeben	**dee**-zehs geh-**pehk owf**-geh-ben

When is the first/	Wann ist der erste/	vahn ist dehr **ehr**-
next/last train to...?	nächste/letzte Zug nach...?	steh/**nekhs**-teh/**lehts**-teh tsook nahkh...
Is this a through train?	Ist es ein durchgehender Zug?	ist dahs ine **durkh**-geh-en-der tsook
Will it stop in Bonn?	Hält der Zug in Bonn?	hehlt dehr tsook in bohn
Is there a connection to Frankfurt?	Gibt es einen Anschluß nach Frankfurt?	gipt ehs **ine**-en **ahn**-shlus nahkh **frahnk**-foort
When does it arrive in Frankfurt?	Wann kommt er in Frankfkurt an?	vahn kohmt ehr in **frahnk**-foort ahn

Is there ... on the train?	*Hat der Zug...?*	*haht deer tsook*
a dining car	einen Speisewagen	**ine**-en **shpye**-zeh-vaa-gen
a sleeping car	einen Schlafwagen	**ine**-en **shlaaf**-vah-gen
a through coach to Bern	einen Kurswagen nach Bern	**ine**-en **koors**-vaa-gen nahkh behrn

From which platform does the train to Mainz leave?	Auf welchem Bahnsteig fährt der Zug nach Mainz ab?	owf **vehl**-khem **baan**-shtike fehrt dehr tsook nahkh mince ahp
On which track does the train from Kiel arrive?	Auf welchem Gleis kommt der Zug aus Kiel an?	owf **vehl**-khem glice komt dehr tsook ows keel ahn

Do you have a timetable?	Haben Sie einen Fahrplan?	**haa**-ben zee **ine**-en **faar**-plaan
Excuse me, is this seat taken?	Entschuldigen Sie, ist der Platz besetzt?	ehnt-**shool**-dee-gen zee, ist dehr plahts beh-**zehtst**

OUT IN THE COUNTRY

Is there a scenic route to...?	Gibt es eine landschaftlich schöne Straße nach...?	gipt ehs **ine**-eh **lahnt**-shahft-likh **shur**-neh **shtrah**-seh naakh
How far is it to...?	Wie weit ist es bis...?	vee vite ist ehs bis
Is there a bus/train from here to...?	Gibt es einen Bus/Zug von hier nach...?	gipt ehs **ine**-nen bus/tsook fohn hear naakh
How long does the trip take?	Wie lange dauert die Fahrt?	vee **lahng**-eh **dow**-ehrt dee fahrt
Can we walk?	Können wir zu Fuß gehen?	**kurn**-nen veer tsoo foos **gay**-en

Where do I find the ...?	*Wo finde ich...?*	*voh* fin-*deh ikh*
beach	den Strand	dehn shtrahnt
bridge	die Brücke	dee **brew**-keh
castle	das Schloß/die Burg	dahs shloss/dee boorg
crossroad	die Kreuzung	dee **kroy**-tsung
caves	die Höhlen	dee **her**-len
farm	den Bauernhof	dehn **bow**-ehrn-hohf
footpath	den Fußweg	dehn **foos**-vehk
forest	den Wald	dehn vahlt
fortress	die Festung	dee **fehs**-tung
garden	den Garten	dehn **gahr**-ten
inn	das Gasthaus	dahs **gahst**-hows
lake	den See	dehn zay
meadow	die Wiese	dee **vee**-seh
path	den Weg	dehn vayk
mountain pass	den Paß	dehn pahs
river	den Fluß/ Strom	dehn fluss/shtroam
road	die Straße	dee **shtrah**-seh
sea	die See/das Meer	dee zay/dahs mare
village	das Dorf	dahs dohrf
vineyard	den Weinberg	dehn **vine**-behrk

CHAPTER TEN

Dining out

Most of the larger cities in German-speaking countries offer an exciting array of cuisine from all over the world. In some cities, finding a traditional restaurant featuring German cooking (**die deutsche Küche**) might be a challenge – but worth the search because the better ones are quite reasonably priced. Traditional German cooking tends to be rich and hearty with generous portions of meat and potatoes. German beer, bread and sausages are arguably the best in the world and even in smaller towns there is a remarkable variety of these, as well as other staples like smoked and pickled meats and fish. In traditional eating places – **Gaststätte**, **Gasthaus** or **Kneipe** – strangers will sometimes share tables. The polite thing to do is to wish the others **Guten Appetit** when they start to eat, and **Auf Wiedersehen** when you or they are leaving.

Is there a restaurant that serves local specialties?	Gibt es ein Restaurant, das einheimische Spezialitäten serviert?	gipt ehs ine res-tow-**rahng**, dahs **ine**-heye-mish-eh shpehts-yah-lee-**tayt**-en zehr-**veert**
Is there a good, not too expensive German restaurant around here?	Gibt es ein gutes, nicht zu teures deutsches Restaurant in der Nähe?	gipt ehs ine goo-tehs nikht tsoo toy-rehs **doy**-ches res-tow-**rahng** in dehr **nay**-eh
Can you recommend an inexpensive restaurant with local/German specialties?	Können Sie mir ein preiswertes Restaurant mit einheimischen/deutschen Spezialitäten empfehlen?	**kern**-en zee meer ine **preyes**-vehrt-es res-two-**rahng** mit ine-heye-mish-en/**doy**-chen shpehts-yah-lee-**tayt**-en emp-**fayl**-en

What's the name of the restaurant?	Wie heißt das Restaurant?	vee heyst dahs rehs-to-**rahng**
How do you get there?	Wie kommt man dahin?	vee komt mahn dah-**hin**
Do I need a reservation?	Brauche ich eine Vor-bestellung?	**brow**-kheh ikh **ine**-eh **for**-beh-shteh-lung
I'd like to reserve a table for four.	Ich möchte einen Tisch für vier Personen reservieren lassen.	ikh **murkh**-teh **ine**-en tish fewr feer pehr-**zoa**-nen reh-zehr-**vee**-ren **lah**-sen
We'll come at eight o'clock.	Wir kommen um acht Uhr.	veer **kom**-men um ahkht oor
Could we have a table...?	*Können wir einen Tisch...haben?*	kurn-*nen veer ine-en tish...**baa**-ben*
in the corner	in der Ecke	in dehr **ehk**-eh
by the window	am Fenster	ahm **fehn**-stehr
outside	im Freien	im **fry**-en
on the terrace	auf der Terrasse	owf dehr teh-**rahs**-seh
in a smoking/non-smoking area	in der Raucher/Nicht-raucherecke	in dehr **rowkh**-ehr/**nikht**-rowkh-ehr-eh-keh
Waiter/Waitress, the menu, please.	Herr Ober/Fräulein, die Speisekarte, bitte.	hehr **oh**-behr/**froy**-line, dee **shpye**-zeh-kahr-teh, **bit**-teh

Let's order

Waiter/Waitress: (Kellner/in):	Would you like to order now? Möchten Sie jetzt bestellen? (**murkh**-ten zee yehtzt beh-**sthehl**-len)
Guest: (Gast):	What is your local specialty? Was ist Ihre hiesige Spezialität? (vahs ist **ee**-reh **hee**-zee-geh shpeh-tsyah-lee-**tayt**)
Waiter/Waitress:	I recommend roast duck. Ich empfehle Ihnen Entenbraten. (ikh ehm-**pfay**-leh **ee**-nen **ehn**-ten-braa-ten)
Guest:	Fine, I'll take that. Schön, das nehme ich. (shurn, dahs **nay**-meh ikh)

Waiter/Waitress:	Would you like something to drink?
	Möchten Sie etwas zu trinken?
	(**murkh**-ten zee **eht**-vahs tsoo **trin**-ken)
Guest:	Yes, please bring me a glass of beer/wine/mineral
	water.
	Ja, bringen Sie mir bitte ein Glas Beer/Wein/
	Mineralwasser.
	(yaa, **brin**-gen zee meer **bit**-eh ine glaas beer/vine/
	mi-neh-**raal**-vahs-er)

EATING AND DRINKING PLACES

Eating keeps the stomach and soul together (**Essen hält Magen und Seele zusammen**). That, in a nutshell, symbolizes the importance German-speaking people attach to good food and drink. Numerous eating establishments will provide you with the opportunity to share this wonderful experience.

Bierhalle (**beer**-hahl-eh): The most famous *Bierhalle* is in Munich where thousands of people celebrate Oktoberfest each year. But *Bierhallen* are open all year long and can be found anywhere. Beer is served from the tap (*vom Hahn*) usually in half or one litre glasses. Basic hot meals, cold cuts, sausages and salads are served.

Bierstube (**beer**-shtoo-beh): Much smaller and cosier (*gemütlich*), the *Bierstube* is more like an English pub and offers local beers, many other alcoholic beverages and a very limited variety of hot and cold dishes.

Café: The Café represents a very old tradition in German-speaking countries. After a Sunday walk (*Spaziergang*) people will enjoy a cup of coffee or tea with an assortment of pastries, ice cream, snacks or other soft drinks. The Swiss version is called tearoom (**Teeraum**), and the Austrian equivalent *Kaffeehaus*. Vienna, in particular, is famous for its long and rich tradition of *Kaffeehauskultur*. For centuries poets, philosophers, politicians, the rich and famous and anyone who enjoyed conversation and laughter congregated there.

Konditorei (kon-dee-toh-**rye**): The Konditorei specializes in numerous sinful concoctions full of thousands of calories and pleasures. A myriad of multilayered cakes (*Torte*) and pastries awaits you, too hard to resist. But there are now also opportunities for the more calorie-conscious traveller to indulge in flavored milk drinks and yogurt dishes.

Gasthaus/Gasthof (**gahst**-hows/**gahst**-hohf): This rustic inn is usually found in villages and small towns and features local specialties, home-style cooking and animated conversation (if you speak some German). Bed and breakfast is sometimes offered, or information about where to find it.

Kneipe (**knye**-peh): The *Kneipe* or pub is similar to a *Bierstube* and is common throughout Germany. It is the glue of the neighborhood that has served for centuries as a meeting place for local residents to escape the trials and tribulations of everyday life. Those frequented by students are called *Studentenkneipen* and serve as local hangouts to discuss and solve all the problems of the world. In Berlin it represents a culure of its own and is found at most corners of the city.

Raststätte/Rasthof (**rahst**-shteht-eh/**rahst**-hohf): A roadside restaurant found right off the expressway (*Autobahn*), it offers a service station, facilities and often lodgings for the tired traveller. The variety of food is extensive and the motorist is treated these days to a vast array of culinary experiences and shopping adventures.

Ratskeller (**rahts**-kehl-ler): The Ratskeller again follows an old tradition, where members of the local council used to meet to enjoy a nice meal and drink after a hard day's work. Much care has been taken to restore and preserve these old places, often the best environments to sample local specialties.

Restaurant (rehs-toh-**rahnt**): These restaurants usually feature a great variety of local cuisine as well as international dishes. Also called *Gaststätte*, they will cater to the customer in smaller towns who is accustomed to more personalized service.

Schnellbuffet (**shnehl**-bew-fay): Establishments such as McDonald's have made tremendous inroads all over Europe. Fast food has become very popular because more and more travellers and local people don't have the time to indulge in a leisurely meal.

Schnellimbiß (**shnehl**-im-bis): This snackbar is often a small stand, located outside, serving beer and a great choice of sausages such as fried sausage (*Bratwurst*), frankfurters (*Knackwurst*), curry sausage (*Currywurst)* or any other local specialty. They are also called *Würstestand* in Austria and offer French fries (**pommes frites**) and other meat snacks.

    Weinstube (**vine**-shtoo-beh): Similar to the ***Bierstube***, it is a cosy type of restaurant found in the wine-producing districts where you can sample new wine with simple hot dishes and snacks. The Austrian as well as Swiss versions serve their own local and often potent wines, identified by a wreath of vines over the door. The Viennese suburb of ***Grinzing*** is famous for its colorful and cosy ***Heurige*** (a wine that is literally of this year).

Mealtimes

Frühstück (**frew**-shrewk): Breakfast is served from 7 to 10 a.m. and is usually included in the price of the hotel. It can range from a simple "continental breakfast" (bread, butter, jam, coffee or tea) to more elaborate buffets, including fresh fruit, eggs, cereal and cold cuts which tend to be very expensive.

Mittagessen (**mit**-taak-ehs-sen): Lunch from 12 to 2 p.m. is the main meal of the day. No restaurants or other more formal eating establishments will offer meals after that time. The meal usually consists of a hearty selection of soup, meat or fish, and vegetable.

Kaffee (**kah**-fay): This afternoon snack from 3 to 5 p.m. is a weekend tradition, especially on Sundays. After an extensive walk, customers will enjoy stopping at the nearest ***Café*** or ***Konditorei*** to have a snack consisting of coffee or tea, cake and pasteries, but can also include something more substantial like bread, cheese and cold cuts. In Austria this meal goes by the name of ***Vesperbrot***, and in Switzerland it is called ***Zvieri***.

Abendessen (**AA**-behnt-ehs-sen): Dinner is served from 6 to 9 p.m. and is generally a light meal. It usually consists of a variety or rye bread and pumpernickel and an assortment of cheese, cold cuts, fish (smoked and canned) and salads. In most restaurants, however, you will still find full-course meals in the evening. Some large restaurants serve until 10 or 11 p.m. After this, it's usually cold snacks or hot sausages only.

IN THE RESTAURANT

English	German	Pronunciation
Did you make a reservation?	Haben Sie schon einen Tisch bestellt?	**hah**-ben zee shohn **ine**-en tish beh-**shtehlt**
How many people?	Wieviele Personen?	vee-**feel**-eh pehr-**zoh**-nen
Would you like to sit here or by the window?	Möchten Sie hier oder am Fenster sitzen?	**murkh**-ten zee heer **oh**-dehr ahm **fens**-tehr **zit**-sen
Do you need a high chair?	Brauchen Sie einen Kinderstuhl?	**brow**-khen zee **ine**-en **kin**-der-shtool
Waiter/Waitress, the menu please.	Herr Ober/ Fräulein, die Speisekarte, bitte.	hehr **oh**-ber/**froy**-line, dee **shpye**-zeh-kahr-teh, **bit**-teh
What would you recommend?	Was würden Sie empfehlen?	vahs **vewr**-den zee ehm-**pfay**-len
Do you have local dishes?	Haben Sie hiesige Gerichte?	**haa**-ben zee **hee**-zee-geh geh-**rikh**-teh
Today I recommend...	Heute ist... zu empfehlen.	**hoy**-teh ist... tsoo ehm-**pfay**-len
Would you like to order drinks?	Möchten Sie Getränke bestellen?	**murkh**-ten zee geh-**trehn**-keh beh-**shtel**-en
Are you ready to order?	Haben Sie schon gewählt?	**haa**-ben zee shohn geh-**vaylt**
We're ready to order now.	Wir möchten bestellen.	veer **murkh**-ten beh-**shtehl**-len
We need more time.	Wir brauchen mehr Zeit.	veer **brow**-khen mehr tsite
What would you like?	Was wünschen Sie?	vahs **vewn**-khen zee
To begin with I'd like...	Als erstes möchte ich...	ahls **ehr**-stes **murkh**-teh ikh
Next...	Als nächstes...	ahls **naykh**-stehs
and finally...	und zum Schluß...	unt tsoom shlus
Thank you, that's all.	Danke, das wäre alles.	**dahn**-keh, dahs **veh**-reh **aa**-lehs
Will it take long?	Wird es lange dauern?	virt ehs **lahn**-geh **dow**-ehrn
We're in a hurry.	Wir haben es eilig.	veer **haa**-ben ehs **eye**-likh

Problems

The tablecloth isn't clean.	Das Tischtuch is nicht sauber.	dahs **tish**-tookh ist nikht **zow**-behr
This is dirty.	Das ist schmutzig.	dahs ist **shmut**-sikh

The food is...	*Das Essen ist...*	*dahs ess-en ist*
cold	kalt	kahlt
not very hot	nicht sehr heiß	nikht zayr heyess
not even warm	nicht einmal warm	nikht **ine**-mahl varhm

There is too much fat in it.	Da ist zu viel Fett drin.	dah ist tsoo feel feht drin

This is too...	*Dies ist zu...*	*dees ist tsoo*
salty	salzig	**zahlts**-iskh
dried out	dürr	dewr
sweet	süss	zews
sour	sauer	**zow**-er
bitter	bitter	**bit**-ter

The meat is...	*Das Fleisch ist...*	*dahs fleyesh ist*
overdone	zu stark gebraten	tsoo shtahrk ge-**braat**-en
too tough	zu zäh	tsoo tsay
too rare	zu roh	tsoo roh

The milk is sour.	Die Milch hat einen Stich.	die milkh haht **ine**-en shtikh
The butter isn't fresh.	Die Butter ist nicht frisch.	die **but**-tehr ist nikht frish
I want to talk to the head waiter.	Ich möchte mit dem Oberkellner sprechen.	ikh **merkh**-teh mit daym **oh**-behr-kel-nehr **shprehk**-en
I didn't order this.	Das habe ich nicht bestellt.	dahs **haa**-be ikh nikht beh-shtehlt
There must be a mistake.	Es muß ein Irrtum sein.	ehs mus ine **eer**-toom zine

THE BILL (DIE RECHNUNG)

The bill, please.	Die Rechnung, bitte.	dee **rehkh**-nung, **bit**-teh
May I pay?	Darf ich zahlen?	dahrf ikh **tsaa**-len
We'd like separate checks.	Wir möchten getrennt bezahlen.	veer **murkh**-ten geh-**trehnt** beh-**tsaa**-len
Is service included?	Ist die Bedienung inbegriffen?	ist dee beh-**dee**-nung **in**-beh-grif-en
That is for you.	Das ist für Sie.	dahs ist fewr zee
The meal was delicious.	Das Essen war vorzüglich.	dahs **ehs**-sen vahr for-**tsewg**-likh
And the service was excellent.	Und die Bedienung war ausgezeichnet.	unt dee beh-**dee**-nung wahr **ows**-geh-tsyekh-neht

Although tips are included in the bill (15 percent), most customers will round up the bill to the next number.

Reading the menu

Most restaurants display a menu (**Speisekarte**) outside. Here is a list of common menu terms and phrases:

Tageskarte	**taa**-gehs-kahr-teh	daily menu
Tagesmenü/ gedeck	**taa**-gehs-meh-new/ geh-dehk	set meal of the day
Tagesgericht	**taa**-gehs-geh-rikht	dish of the day
Tagessuppe	**taa**-gehs-zoop-peh	soup of the day
Spezialität des Hauses	shpeh-tsyah-li-**tayt** dehs-**how**-zehs	specialty of the house
Hausgemacht	**hows**-geh-mahkht	homemade
Extraaufschlag	**ehk**-strah-owf-shlahk	additional charge
Im Preis inbegriffen	im price **in**-beh-gri-ffen	included in the price
Alle Preise sind inklusive Bedienung und Mehrwertsteuer (Mwst).	**ah**-leh **prye**-zeh zint in-cloo-**zee**-veh beh-**dee**-nung unt **mehr**-vehrt-shtoy-er	all prices include service and value-added tax.

WHAT'S ON THE MENU?

Here are some menu headings you'll find in most restaurants:

Vorspeisen und	**for**-shpye-sen unt	appetizers and
kalte Platten	**kahl**-teh **plaht**-ten	cold cuts
Suppen und	**zoop**-pen unt	soups and
Eintopfgerichte	**ine**-topf-geh-rikh-teh	stews
Hauptgerichte	**howpt**-geh-rikh-teh	main dishes
Fleischgerichte	**flyshe**-geh-rikh-teh	meat dishes
Fisch und	fish unt **may**-rehs-	fish and seafood/
Meeresfrüchte/	frewkh-teh/	from the sea
vom Meer	fom mayr	
Wild und Geflügel	vilt unt geh-**flew**-gel	game and poultry
Beilagen, Neben-und	**bye**-laa-gen, **nay**-ben-	accompaniments,
Kleingerichte	unt **kline**-geh-rikh-teh	side and small dishes
Salate	zah-**laa**-teh	salads
Gemüsegerichte	geh-**mew**-zeh-geh-	vegetable dishes
	rikh-teh	
Reis-und	rice unt kahr-**tof**-el-	rice and potato
Kartoffelgerichte	geh-rikh-teh	dishes
Teigwaren und	**tike**-vaa-ren unt	pasta and
Nudelgerichte	**noo**-del-geh-rikh-teh	noodle dishes
Eierspeisen	**eye**-er-shpye-zen	egg dishes
Wurst und Käse	voorst unt **kay**-zeh	sausages and cheese
Nachttisch/Süß-	**nahkh**-tish/**zews**-	desserts
speisen	shpye-zen	
Gebäck	geh-**behk**	pastries
Eis/Glacé	ice/**glah**-say	ice cream
Obst und Nüsse	opst unt **news**-seh	fruit and nuts
Getränke	geh-**trehn**-keh	beverages/drinks
Wein und Bier	vine unt beer	wine and beer
Andere alkoholische	**ahn**-deh-reh-	other alcoholic
Getränke	ahl-koh-**hoh**-lish-eh	drinks
	geh-**trehn**-keh	
Alkoholfreie	ahl-koh-hol-**frye**-eh	nonalcoholic drinks
Getränke	geh-**trehn**-keh	
Warme Getränke	**vaar**-meh	hot beverages
	geh-**trehn**-keh	

Methods of cooking and preparation

Nach Pariser Art	Parisien style
Nach Ungarischer Art	Hungarian style (with paprika, etc.)
Nach Hausfrauenart	*Sauce bonne femme* (with apples and onions)
Nach Jägerart	In the hunter's style (sauce chasseur - a blend of mushrooms, vegetable and wine)
Hühnerbrust Kiever Art	Breast of Chicken Kiev

Methods of cooking

Meat

gebacken	geh-**bah**-ken	baked
geröstet	geh-**rurs**-tet	roasted
geschmort	geh-**shmohrt**	braised or stewed
gekocht	geh-**kokht**	boiled
in der Pfanne gebraten	in dehr **pfah**-neh geh-**braa**-ten	pan-fried
im Ofen gebraten	im **oh**-fen geh-**braa**-ten	oven-roasted
gegrillt	geh-**grilt**	grilled, broiled
vom Spieß	fom shpees	from the spit
gedämpft	geh-**dehmpft**	steamed
gefüllt	geh-**fewlt**	stuffed
gut durchgebraten	goot durkh-ge-**braa**-ten	well done
mittel	**mit**-tel	medium
blutig	**bloo**-tikh	rare, underdone

Fish

mariniert	mah-ri-**neert**	marinated
gebacken	geh-**bah**-ken	baked
geräuchert	geh-**roy**-khert	smoked
paniert	pah-**neert**	breaded

TYPICAL DISHES

Here are some well-known dishes served in Germany, Austria and Switzerland.

Appetizers

Ich hätte gern...	*ikh* heh-*teh gehrn*	*I'd like to have...*
eine Vorspeise	**ine**-eh **fohr**-shpy-seh	an appetizer
Appetithäppchen	ah-peh-**teet**-hehp-khyen	canapés
Artischockenherzen	ahr-ti-**shok**-en-herts-en	hearts of artichokes
in Öl	in erl	in oil
Bismarckhering	**bis**-mahrk-hay-ring	marinated herring with onions
Bückling	**bewk**-ling	kipper, bloater
Fleischpastete	**fleyish**-pahs-tay-teh	meat pie, meat loaf
Froschschenkel	**frosh**-shehnk-el	frog's legs
Gänseleberpastete	**gehn**-zeh-lay-ber-pahs-tay-teh	goose liver paté
Geräucherte Gänsebrust	geh-**roykh**-ehr-teh **gehn**-zeh-brust	smoked breast of goose
Gefüllte Champignons	geh-**fewl**-teh shahm-pin-**yongs**	stuffed mushrooms
Käsehäppchen	**kay**-zeh-hehp-khen	bits of cheeses
Krabben	**krahb**-en	tiny shrimps
Lachs	lahks	very thin slices of smoked salmon
Languste	lahn-**gus**-teh	spiny lobster

If you feel like a little something to whet your appetite, choose carefully: German appetizers can be filling. Starters may also be listed on the menu under *Kleine Gerichte/Warme Vorspeisen* or *Kalte Platten.*

Ich hätte gern...	ikh heh-teh gehrn	I'd like to have...
Makrele	mah-**kray**-leh	mackerel (usually smoked)
Matjeshering	**mah**-tyehs-hay-ring	a young white, salted herring usually served with rye bread or new potatoes
Rehpastete	**ray**-pahs-tay-teh	venison paté
Schinken	**shink**-en	ham
Schnecken	**shnehk**-en	snails
Spargelspitzen	**shpahr**-gel-shpit-sen	asparagus tips
Wurstsalat	**voorst**-zah-laat	cold cuts chopped and served with onions and oil
Verschiedene kleine Vorspeisen	fer-**shee**-deh-neh kli-neh for-**shpeye**-zen	various little appetizers (hors d'oeuvres)

MEATS

Germans are very fond of meats and offer them boiled, fried, roasted, served hot or cold or all of these together. You can often order a monster meat platter which might also include ham or tongue and a whole range of sausages, with or without sauerkraut and other garnishes (dumplings and red cabbage are very popular). On some menus, you will see subheadings **vom Schwein**, **vom Kalb** and **vom Rind** (from the pig, from the calf, from beef) under which the different dishes are grouped.

Bauernomelett	**bow**-ehrn-om-let	bacon and onion omelette
Bauernschmaus	**bow**-ehrn-shmowss	sauerkraut with smoked pork, sausages, dumplings and potatoes
Bauernwurst	**bow**-ehrn-voorst	pork sausage with mustard seeds and peppercorns
Berliner Buletten	behr-**leen**-er bul-**eht**-en	fried meat balls, Berlin style
Bratwurst	**braat**-voorst	fried sausage

deutsches Beefsteak	doy-ches beef-stayk	Salisbury steak, hamburger
Eisbein	ice-bine	pig's knuckle
Gulasch	goo-lahsh	beef stew with spicy paprika gravy
Hackbraten	hahk-braat-en	meat loaf
Hammelbraten	hahm-el-braat-en	roast lamb
Hammelkeule/	hahm-el-koyl-eh/	leg of lamb
Hammelschlegel	hahm-el-shlay-gel	
Hammelrippchen	hahm-el-rip-khen	lamb chops
Holsteiner Schnitzel	hol-shteyen-er shnits-el	breaded veal cutlet, topped with fried egg
Kalbsbraten	kahlps-braat-en	roast veal
Klöße	klerss-eh	meat balls
Kohlroulade	kohl-roo-laad-en	stuffed cabbage
Leber	lay-ber	liver
Rinderbraten	rind-er-braat-en	roast beef
Rouladen	roo-laad-en	vegetables rolled up in thin slices of beef or veal
Sauerbraten	zow-ehr-braat-en	marinated pot roast in a spicy brown gravy
Schlachtplatte	shlahkht-plaht-eh	mixed sausages and cold meats
Schnitzel	shnits-el	cutlet (usually veal)
Schweinskotelett	shveyens-kot-let	pork chop
Speck	shpehk	bacon
Wiener Schnitzel	veen-er shnits-el	breaded veal cutlet
Zigeuner Schnitzel	tsee-goyn-er shnits-el	veal or pork cutlet in a sharp sauce

POULTRY AND GAME

Goose and duck are very popular in German-speaking Europe. In Catholic Austria and parts of Germany, goose is very widely eaten on St. Martin's Day in November. It is known as **Martingansl**. Berliners, too, appreciate a well-roasted goose, a **Weihnachtsgans** (Christmas goose). During the autumn hunting season, many restaurants feature **Wild** (game). Some even modify their decor with hunting motifs.

Backhuhn	**bahk**-hoon	fried chicken
Hühnerkeule	**hewh**-nehr-koy-leh	drumstick
Brathuhn	**braat**-hoon	roast chicken
Entenbraten	**ehnt**-en-brah-ten	roast duck
Fasan	fah-**zaan**	pheasant
Gänsebraten	**gehn**-zeh-braa-ten	roast goose
Hähnchen	**hayn**-khen	small chicken
Hasenbraten	**haa**-zen- braa-ten	roast hare
Hasenpfeffer	**haa**-zen-pfeh-fer	spicy rabbit stew
Hirschbraten	**heersh**-braa-ten	venison
Kaninchen	kah-neen-khen	rabbit
Rebhuhn	**rayp**-hoon	partridge
Rehrücken	**ray**-rewk-en	saddle of venison
Taube	**tow**-beh	pigeon, dove, squab
Truthahn	**troot**-hahn	turkey
Wiener Backhendl	**vee**-nehr **bakh**-hen-del	Southern fried chicken–Viennese style
Wildbraten	**vilt**-braa-ten	roast venison
Wildschweinrücken	**vilt**-shvine-rewk-en	saddle of wild boar

FISH, SEAFOOD

Is the fish fresh?	Ist der Fisch frisch?	ist dehr fish frish
What is the catch of the day?	Was ist der Tagesfang?	vaas ist dehr **taa**-ges-fahng
Does the fish have many bones?	Hat der Fisch viele Gräten?	haht dehr fish **fee**-leh **gray**-ten
Can you remove the fishbone for me?	Können Sie mir die Gräte entfernen?	**kern**-en zee meer dee **gray**-teh ent-**fehr**-nen

The following is a list of fish commonly found on menus. Often the name of the lake or sea precedes the fish, as in **Bodensee Dorsch** (Lake Constance cod).

Aal	aal	eel
Austern	**ow**-stern	oysters
Barsch	bahrsh	(lake) perch
Dorsch	dorsh	cod
Fischfrikadellen	**fish**-fri-kah-deh-len	fish dumplings (croquettes)

Forelle	foh-**reh**-leh	trout
Flunder	**flun**-dehr	flounder
Haifischsteak	**heye**-fish-shtayk	shark steak
Hecht	hekht	pike
Heilbutt	**heyle**-but	halibut
Hering	**hay**-ring	herring
Hummer	**hum**-mehr	lobster
Jakobsmuscheln	**yaa**-kops-mush-eln	scallops
Junger Hecht	**yung**-ehr hekht	pickerel
Kabeljau	**kaa**-bel-yow	cod
Karpfen	**kahr**-pfen	carp
Krabben	**krah**-ben	shrimp, prawn
Muscheln	**mush**-eln	clams, mussels
Rotbarsch	**roht**-bahrsh	red sea bass
Schellfisch	**shehl**-fish	haddock
Schwertfisch	**shvayrt**-fish	swordfish
Seebarsch	**zay**-bahrsh	sea bass
Seezunge	**zay**-tsung-eh	sole
Steinbutt	**shteyen**-buht	turbot
Tintenfisch	**tint**-en-fish	squid

Unless you have these fish either smoked or marinated (**geräuchert, mariniert**), your waiter may ask you:

How would you like this fish?	*Wie möchten Sie den Fisch?*	*vee **murk**-ten zee dehn fish*
with butter, lemon and almond	mit Butter, Zitrone und Mandeln	mit **butt**-er, tsi-**troh**-neh unt **mahn**-deln
with caper sauce	mit Kapernsauce	mit **kaa**-pehrn-zoh-sseh
baked	gebacken	geh-**bah**-ken
fried	gebraten	geh-**braa**-ten
deep fried	in schwimmendem Fett gebacken	in **shvim**-en-dem feht ge-**bah**-ken
sautéed	in Butter geschwenkt	in **but**-er geh-**shvehngkt**
grilled	gegrillt	geh-**gtrilt**
steamed	gedämpft	geh-**dehmpft**

81

VEGETABLES

I eat only vegetables.	Ich esse nur Gemüse.	ikh **ess**-eh noor geh-**mewz**-eh
I am a vegetarian.	Ich bin Vegetarier.	ikh bin veh-geh-**taar**-ee-er
What kind of vegetables are there?	Was für Gemüse gibt es?	vahs fewr ge-**mewz**-eh geept ehs

Blumenkohl	**bloom**-en-kohl	cauliflower
Bohnen	**bohn**-en	beans
Braunkohl	**brown**-kohl	broccoli
Erbsen	**ehrps**-en	peas
Gemischtes Gemüse	geh-**misht**-ehs ge-**mewz**-eh	beans mixed vegetables
Grüne Bohnen	**grewn**-eh BOHN-en	green beans
Gurken	**goork**-en	cucumbers
Karotten	kahr-**ot**-en	carrots
Knoblauch	**knohp**-lowkh	garlic
Kohl	kohl	cabbage
Kukuruz (Austria)	**kook**-oor-oots	corn, maize
Lauch	lowkh	leeks
Mais	mice	corn, maize
Pilze	**pilts**-eh	mushrooms
Rosenkohl	**rohz**-en-kohl	brussel sprouts
Rotkohl	**roht**-kohl	red cabbage
Spargelspitzen	**shpaarg**-el-shpits-en	asparagus tips
Spinat	shpeen-**aat**	spinach
Tomaten	to-**maat**-en	tomatoes
Zwiebeln	**tsveeb**-eln	onions

DESSERTS

Germany is the perfect country for indulging your sweet tooth. Menus will usually list desserts under various different headings: **Nachtische**, **Nachspeise**, or **Süßspeise**. In Vienna, you will almost certainly hear the question **Mit Schlag?** (With whipped cream?).

Here are a few basic desserts you will find, usually as a combination with fruit or in different flavors:

-auflauf	**owf**-lowf	soufflé
-eis/-glacé	ice/-glah-**seh**	ice cream

-gebäck	geh-**behk**	pastry
-kompott	kom-**pot**	compote
-kuchen	**koo**-khen	cake
-pudding	**pud**-ding	pudding
-strudel	**shtroo**-del	delicate, thin, flaky pastry
-torte	**tor**-te	tart or layer cake

Some notable traditional desserts:

Apfelrösti	**ahp**-fel-rurs-tee	apple and bread slices fried in butter
Apfelstrudel	**ahp**-fel-shtroo-del	strudel filled with sliced apples, raisins, nuts and jam
Berliner	behr-**lee**-ner	doughnut filled with raspberry
Linzertorte	**lin**-tser-tor-teh	crushed almond cake with raspberry
Mohnkuchen	**mohn**-koo-khen	poppy seed cake
Sachertorte	**zahkh**-er-tor-teh	apricot jam layer cake with chocolate icing and filling (famous Viennese specialty)
Schwarzwälder Kirschtorte	**shvarts**-vehl-der-**keersh**-tor-teh	Black Forest cake creamy, chocolate layer cake with cherries and cherry brandy

WINE AND BEER

Germany produces mostly white wines, the most famous of which come from the Rhine and Mosel River vallyes. The better-quality German wines are usually sweet and are classified as **Qualitätswein**. These wines can be enjoyed by themselves or as a dessert wine. **Deutscher Tafelwein** (German table wine) is usually a blend of the more common dryer wines. Germans are also fond of sparkling wine, called **Schaumwein**, and produce some of the best anywhere.

| May I see the wine list, please? | Die Weinkarte, bitte. | dee **vine**-kahr-teh, **bit**-teh |

Can you recommend a good local wine?	Können Sie mir einen guten Wein aus dieser Gegend empfehlen?	**kur**-nen zee meer **ine**-en **goo**-ten vine ows **dee**-zer **gay**-gehnt ehm-**pfay**-len
Is this wine...	*Ist dieser Wein...*	*ist* dee-*zer vine*
(very) dry	(sehr) trocken	(zehr) **troh**-ken
(a little) sweet	(etwas) süß	(**eht**-vahs) zews
light/heavy	leicht/schwer	lyekht/shvehr
full-bodied	vollmundig	**vol**-mun-dikh
I'd like a glass/bottle/ carafe of ...	*Ich möchte ein Glas/ eine Flasche/eine Karaffe...*	*ikh **murkh**-teh ine glaas/**ine**-eh **flahs**-eh/ **ine**-eh **kah**-rah-feh*
house wine	Hauswein	**hows**-vine
white wine	Weißwein	**vice**-vine
red wine	Rotwein	**roht**-vine
rosé	Rosé/Schillerwein	roh-**zay**/**shil**-ler-vine
sparkling wine	Sekt	zehkt
Please bring me another...	Bringen Sie mir bitte noch...	**brin**-gen zee meer **bit**-teh nohkh

Beer

Germany is extremely proud of its beer and offers an amazing variety. Even small towns have breweries. There are two main categories of beer: **helles** which is light in color, and **dunkles** which is dark. Ordering is very easy: *Ein Bier, bitte* (A beer, please) or...

I'd like a small/large glass of beer.	Ich hätte gern ein kleines/großes Bier.	ikh **heht**-teh gehrn ine kline-es/grohs-ehs beer

Other beverages

I'd like a/an...	*Ich hätte gern ...*	*ikh heht-teh gehrn*
mineral water	ein Mineralwasser	ine mi-neh-**raal**-vahs-ser
fruit juice	einen Obstsaft	**ine**-en **opst**-zahft
apple juice	einen Apfelsaft	**ine**-en **ahp**-fehl-zahft
orange juice	einen Orangensaft	**ine**-en oh-**rahn**-zhen-zahft
lemonade	eine Limonade	**ine**-eh lee-mo-**naa**-deh
iced tea	einen Eistee	**ine**-en **ice**-tay

Other beverages

I'd like a/an...	Ich hätte gern ...	ikh heht-teh gehrn
hot chocolate	eine heiße Schokolade	ine-eh hice-seh sho-ko-laa-deh
cup/pot of coffee	eine Tasse/ein Kännchen Kaffee	ine-eh tahs-eh/ine kehn-shen kah-feh
with cream	mit Sahne	mit zaa-neh
black/decaffeinated coffee	einen schwarzen/ koffeinfreien Kaffee	ine-en shvahrt-sen/ kof-feh-een-frey-en kah-feh
tea with lemon/milk	einen Tee mit Zitrone/ Milch	ine-en tay mit tsi-troh-neh/milkh
herbal tea	einen Kräutertee	ine-en kroy-ter-tay

CHAPTER ELEVEN

Medical emergencies

Medical facilities and services in Germany, Switzerland and Austria are easily accessible, modern and efficient. To be at ease, make sure your health insurance policy covers any illness or accident while on holiday. If not, ask your insurance representative, automobile association or travel agent for details of special health insurance. For prescription drugs, you need an **Apotheke** (pharmacy). For toilet articles, film, household articles and patent medicines, you should go to a **Drogerie**. Many pharmacies also carry non-prescription medicines as well as herbal teas. There is an all-night pharmacy in most towns. The address is posted on the door or window of every pharmacy and can be found in the local phone book.

At the pharmacy (Apotheke)

Pharmacist:	How can help you?
(Apotheker):	Womit kann ich Ihnen dienen?
	(**woh**-mit kahn ikh **ee**-nen **dee**-nen)
Traveller:	Do you have something for a cold?
(Reisender):	Haben Sie etwas gegen eine Erkältung?
	(**haab**-en zee **eht**-vahs **gay**-gen **ine**-eh ehr-**kehlt**-ung)
Pharmacist:	Of course. I have something for the day and the night.
	Sicher. Ich habe etwas für den Tag und die Nacht.
	(**sikh**-er. ikh **haa**-beh **eht**-vahs fewr dehn taak unt dee nahkht)

Traveller:	What would you recommend?	
	Was würden Sie empfehlen?	
	(vahs **vur**-den zee ehm-**pfay**-len)	
Pharmacist:	Both to be sure.	
	Beides um sicher zu sein.	
	(**bye**-des uhm **sikh**-er tsoo sine)	

PHARMACY

Where can I find	Wo finde ich die nächste	voh **find**-eh ikh dee
the nearest (all-night)	Apotheke (mit	**naykst**-eh ah-poh-**tayk**-eh
pharmacy?	Nachtdienst)?	(mit **nahkht**-deenst)
At what time does it	Um wieviel Uhr wird	um **vee**-feel oor veert
open/close?	geöffnet/geschlossen?	geh-**erf**-net/
		geh-**shloss**-en

I need something for...	*Ich brauche etwas gegen...*	*ikh* brow-*khe* eht-*vahs gay-gen*
a cold	eine Erkältung	**ine**-eh ehr-**kehl**-tung
a cough	Husten	**hoos**-ten
a fever	Fieber	**fee**-ber
constipation	Verstopfung	fehr-**shtopf**-ung
diarrhea	Durchfall	**doorkh**-fahl
indigestion	Magenverstimmung	**maag**-en-fehr-shtim-ung
a hangover	Kater	**kaht**-er
hay fever	Heuschnupfen	**hoy**-shnupf-en
insomnia	Schlaflosigkeit	**shlaaf**-loh-zikh-kite
headache	Kopfschmerzen	**kopf**-shmer-tsen
a sore throat	Halsschmerzen	hahls-shmehr-tsen
insect bites	Insektenstiche	in-**zehk**-ten-shtikh-eh
motion sickness	Reisekrankheit	**rye**-zeh-krahk-hite
a toothache	Zahnschmerzen	**tsaan**-shmehrts-en
sunburn	Sonnenbrand	**zon**-en-brahnt
a blister	eine Blase	**ine**-eh **blaaz**-eh
a burn	eine Brandwunde	**ine**-eh **brahnt**-vund-eh

Do I need a	Muß ich ein Rezept	muss ikh ine reh-**tsept**
prescription for the	für das Medikament	fewr dahs may-di-kaa-
medicine?	haben?	**ment** haab-en

Is there a German equivalent for this?	Gibt es ein deutsches Äquivalent für dafür?	gipt ehs ine **doytsh**-es ay-kvi-vah-**lent** da-fewr
Is there something similar?	Gibt es etwas Ähnliches?	gipt ehs **eht**-vahs **ayn**-likh-es
Can you fill this presciption for me?	Können Sie dieses Rezept jetzt anfertigen?	**kern**-en zee **dee**-zehs reh-**tsept** yetst **ahn**-fehr-teeg-en
It's urgent.	Es ist dringend.	ehs ist **dring**-ent
How long will it take?	Wie lange wird es dauern?	vee **lahng**-eh veert ehs **dow**-ehrn
I'll wait.	Ich warte darauf	ikh **vaart**-eh dah-**rowf**
When can I pick it up?	Wann kann ich es abholen?	vahn kahn ikh ehs **ahp**-hohl-en
I need...	*Ich brauche...*	*ikh* brow-*kheh*
a contraceptive	ein Verhütungsmittel	ine fehr-**hew**-tungs-mit-tel
a thermometer	einen Thermometer	ine-en ther-mo-**mayt**-er
a pain killer/analgesic	ein Schmerzmittel	ine **shmehrts**-mit-tel
a laxative	ein Abführmittel	ine **ahp**-fewr-mit-tel
adhesive tape	ein Leukoplast	ine **loy**-ko-plahst
an antiseptic	ein Antiseptikum	ine ahn-tee-**zehp**-ti-koom
an antacid	ein Antiacidum	ine ahn-tee-ah-**see**-doom
antiseptic cream	Wundsalbe	**vunt**-zaal-beh
aspirin	Aspirin	ah-spee-**reen**
band-aids	Heftplaster	**hehft**-pflahs-ter
bandages	Verbandzeug	fehr-**bahnt**-tsoyg
contact lenses	Kontaktlinsen	kon-tahkt-lin-zen-
corn plaster	Hühneraugenpflaster	**hew**-nehr-ow-gen-pflahs-ter
cotton balls	Wattebäusche	**vah**-teh-boysh-eh
cough drops/syrup	Hustenbonbons/-saft	**hoos**-ten-bong-bongs/-zahft
disinfectant	Desinfektionsmittel	**deh**-sin-fehk-**tsiohns**-mit-el
eardrops	Ohrentropfen	**ohr**-en-trop-fen
eyedrops	Augentropfen	**ow**-gen-trop-fen

I need...	Ich brauche...	ikh brow-kheh .
a first-aid kit	einen Verbandkasten	ine-en vehr-bahnt-kahst-en
insect repellent/spray	Insektizid	in-zehk-ti-tseet
iodine	Jod	yoht
mouthwash	Mundwasser	munt-vahs-er
nose drops	Nasentropfen	naa-zen-trop-fen
sanitary napkins	Damenbinden	daa-men-bin-den
sleeping pills	Schlaftabletten	shlaaf-tah-bleht-ten
talcum powder	Talkumpuder	tahlk-um-pood-er
tampons	Tampons	tahm-pongs
throat lozenges	Halspastillen	hahls-pahs-til-en
tranquillizers	ein Beruhigungsmittel	ine beh-roo-ee-gungs-mit-el
vitamins	Vitamine	vee-taa-meen-eh

Modern homeopathy has been popular in Germany for many years. You will, therefore, see many homeopathic pharmacies.

Is there a homeopathic pharmacy here?	Gibt es hier eine homöopathische Apotheke?	gipt ehs heer ine-eh hah-mer-oh-paa-ti-sheh ah-po-tayk-eh
Do you have any book on medicinal herbs?	Haben Sie ein Kräuterbuch?	haab-en zee ine kroy-tehr-bookh
Do you have any herbal tea?	Haben Sie Kräutertee?	haab-en zee kroyt-er-tay
I need a doctor (right away).	Ich brauche (sofort) einen Arzt.	ikh brow-kheh (zoh-fort) ine-nen ahrtst
I think I am sick.	Ich glaube, ich bin krank.	ikh glowb-eh, ikh bin krahnk
I need a doctor.	Ich brauche einen Artzt.	ikh brow-kheh ine-nen ahrtst
Can you get me a doctor?	Können Sie mir einen Arzt holen?	kur-nen zee meer ine-nen ahrts hoh-len

In search of a doctor

If there is an emergency in your hotel or **Pension** (guest house) the staff will be able to put you in touch with one. If not, then you can call the **ärztlicher Notdienst** (emergency medical service), listed at the beginning of every telephone directory. Otherwise the **Fremdenverkehrsamt** (tourist information office) should be able to refer you to a doctor. Doctors' office hours in Germany are usually from 10 a.m. to 12 noon and from 4 to 6 p.m., except Wednesday, Saturday and Sunday.

My wife doesn't feel well.	Meine Frau fühlt sich nicht wohl.	**mine**-neh frow fewlt sikh nikht wohl
Is there a doctor here who speaks English?	Gibt es hier einen Arzt, der Englisch spricht?	gipt ehs heer **ine**-en ahrtst dehr **ehng**-lish shprikht
Could the doctor come to see me here?	Könnte der Arzt mich hier behandeln?	**kurn**-teh dehr ahrtst mikh heer beh-**hahn**-deln
What time can the doctor come?	Wann kann der Arzt kommen?	vahn kahn dehr ahrtst **kom**-men
Can you recommend a/an...?	*Können Sie mir einen ...empfehlen?*	kur-*nen zee meer* ine-en...ehm-pfay-*len*
general practitioner	praktischen Arzt	**prahk**-tish-en ahrtst
gynecologist	Frauenarzt	**frow**-en ahrtst
pediatrician	Kinderarzt	**kin**-der-ahrtst
eye doctor	Augenarzt	**ow**-gen-ahrtst
When are the office hours?	Wann sind die Sprechstunden?	vahn zint dee **shprekh**-shtun-den
Can I have an appointment...?	*Kann ich einen Termin haben...?*	*kahn ikh* ine-*en tehr-meen haa-ben*
as soon as possible/ today/tomorrow	so bald wie möglich/ heute/morgen	zoh bahlt vee **murg**-likh/ **hoy**-teh/**mor**-gen

90

A VISIT TO THE DOCTOR

I'm not feeling well.	Ich fühle mich nicht wohl.	ikh **few**-leh mikh nikht vohl
I'm sick.	Ich bin krank.	ikh bin krahnk
I don't know what's wrong with me.	Ich weiß nicht, was mir fehlt.	ikh vice nikht, vahs meer fehlt
I'm dizzy/nauseated.	Mir ist schwindlig/übel.	meer est **shvihnd**-likh/ew-bel
I have a fever /no fever.	Ich habe Fieber/ kein Fieber.	ikh **haa**-beh **fee**-ber/ kine **fee**-ber
My temperature is 39 degrees.	Ich habe 39 Grad Fieber.	ikh **haa**-beh **noyn**-unt-dri-sikh graht **fee**-ber
I've been vomiting.	Ich habe mich übergeben.	ikh **haa**-beh mikh ew-ber-geh-ben
I've got diarrhea.	Ich habe Durchfall.	ikh **haa**-beh **doorkh**-fahl
I'm constipated.	Ich habe Verstopfung.	ikh **haa**-beh fehr-**shtop**-fung
I feel weak.	Ich fühle mich schwach.	ikh **fewl**-eh mikh shvahkh
I must sit down/ lie down.	Ich muß mich hinsetzen/ hinlegen.	ikh muss mikh **hin**-zets-en/**hin**-layg-en
I'm suffocating here.	Ich ersticke hier.	ikh ehr-**shtik**-eh heer
I need air.	Ich brauche Luft.	ikh **browkh**-eh luft
I can't sleep.	Ich kann nicht schlafen.	ikh kahn nikht **shlaa**-fen
I think this wound is infected.	Ich glaube diese Wunde ist infiziert.	ikh **glowb**-eh **deez**-eh **vund**-eh ist in-fee-**tseert**
Is there any danger of being infected?	Gibt es eine Ansteckungsgefahr?	gipt ehs **ine**-eh **ahn**-steh-kungs-geh-fahr
Do I need an antibiotic?	Brauche ich ein Antibiotikum?	**browkh**-eh ikh ine ahn-tee-bee-**oh**-tee-cum
My...hurts.	*Mein...tut weh.*	*mine... toot vay*
I have...	*Ich habe...*	*ikh* haab-*eh*
an abscess	einen Abszeß	**ine**-en ahps-**tsehs**
asthma	Asthma	**ahst**-mah
backache	Rückenschmerzen	**rewk**-en-shmerts-en
earache	Ohrenschmerzen	**ohr**-en-shmerts-en

My...hurts.	Mein...tut weh.	mine... toot vay
I have...	Ich habe...	ikh haab-eh
a headache	Kopfschmerzen	kopf-shmerts-en
a broken leg	einen Beinbruch	ine-en bine-brukh
a cold	eine Erkältung	ine-eh ehr-kehl-tung
the flu	die Grippe	dee grip-peh
a cough	Husten	hoo-sten
cramps	Krämpfe	krehm-pfeh
indigestion	Verdauungsstörungen	vehr-dow-ungs-shtur-rung-en
a bruise	ein Quetschung	ine-eh kvehtsh-ung
a nosebleed	Nasenbluten	naaz-en-bloot-en
palpitations	Herzklopfen	hehrts-klopf-en
a burn	eine Brandwunde	ine-eh brahnt-vun-deh
a stiff neck	einen steifen Hals	ine-en shtif-en hahls
a stomach ache	Magenschmerzen	mahg-en-shmehrt-sen
a sunstroke	einen Sonnenstich	ine-en zohn-nen-shtikh
a cut	eine Schnittwunde	ine-eh shnit-vund-eh
something in my eye	etwas im Auge	eht-vahs im owg-eh
a lump/swelling	eine Beule/Schwellung	ine-bowl-eh/ shweh-loong
I have difficulty breathing.	Ich habe Atembe-beschwerden.	ikh haa-beh aat-em-bay-shvehrd-en
I have a fracture.	Ich habe einen Knochenbruch	ikh haa-beh ine-en knokh-en-brukh
I have pain in my chest.	Ich habe Schmerzen in der Brust.	ikh haab-eh shmehrt-sen in dehr brust
My blood pressure is high/low.	mein Blutdruck ist zu hoch/niedrig	mine bloot-druk ist tsu hokh/need-rig
I have heart trouble.	Ich bin herzkrank.	ikh bin hehrts-krahnk
I had a heart attack ... years ago.	Ich hatte vor... Jahren einen Herzanfall.	ikh haht-eh for... yaar-en ine-en hehrts-ahn-fahl
I've had this pain for two days.	Seit zwei Tagen habe ich diese Schmerzen	zite tsvye taa-gen haa-beh ikh dee-zeh shmerts-en

I'm (not) allergic to penicillin.	Ich bin gegen Penizillin (nicht)allergisch.	ikh bin **gay**-gen peh-ni-tsil-**leen**-(nikht) ah-**lehr**-gish
I'm a diabetic and take insulin/ this medication.	Ich bin Diabetiker und nehme Insulin/ dieses Medikament.	ikh bin dee-ah-**beh**-ti-ker unt **naym**-eh in-tsu-leen/ **dee**-zehs meh-di-kah-**ment**
I have menstrual pains.	Ich habe Menstruations-beschwerden.	ikh **haa**-beh mehn-stru-ah-**tiohns**-beh-shver-den
I'm six months pregnant.	Ich bin sechs Monate schwanger	ikh bin zehx **moh**-naat-eh **shvahng**-er

PARTS OF THE BODY

My ... hurts.	*Mir tut/tun ... weh.*	*meer toot/toon ... vay*
ankle	der Knöchel	dehr **knur**-khel
appendix	der Blinddarm	dehr **blint**-dahrm
arm	der Arm	dehr ahrm
back	der Rücken	dehr **rew**-ken
bladder	die Blase	dee **blaa**-zeh
bone	die Knochen	dee **knokh**-en
bowels	der Darm	dehr dahrm
breast	die Brust	dee broost
chest	der Brustkorb	dehr **brust**-korp
ear	das Ohr	dahs ohr
elbow	der Ellbogen	dehr **el**-boh-gen
eye	das Auge/die Augen	dahs **ow**-geh/dee **ow**-gen
face	das Gesicht	dahs gej-**zikht**
finger	der Finger	dehr **fin**-ger
foot/feet	der Fuß/die Füße	dehr foos/dee **fews**-seh
gland	die Drüse	dee **drew**-zeh
hand	die Hand	dee hant
head	der Kopf	dehr kopf
heart	das Herz	dahs hehrts
hip	die Hüfte	dee **hewf**-teh
jaw	der Kiefer	dehr **kee**-fer
joint	das Gelenk	dahs geh-**lehnk**
kidney(s)	die Niere(n)	dee **neer**-eh/**neer**-en
knee	das Knie	dahs knee

My...hurts.	Mir tut/tun...web.	meer toot/toon...vay
leg	das Bein	dahs bine
lip	die Lippe	dee **lip**-eh
liver	die Leber	dee **lay**-ber
lung	die Lunge	dee **lung**-eh

What the doctor will say to you

Wo haben Sie Schmerzen?	voh **haa**-ben zee **shmehrt**-sen	Where does it hurt?
Seit wann haben Sie diese Schmerzen?	zite vahn **haa**-ben zee **dee**-zeh **shmehrt**-sen	How long have you had these pains?
Tief atmen und husten, bitte.	teef **aht**-men unt **hoost**-en, **bit**-eh	Breathe deeply and cough, please.
Welche Symptome haben Sie?	**vehl**-kheh **zewmp**-toh-meh **haa**-ben zee	What symptoms do you have?
Welche Medikamente nehmen Sie?	**vehl**-kheh meh-dee-kah-**mehn**-teh **nay**-men zee	What medicines are you taking?
Ziehen Sie sich bitte aus/an.	**tsee**-en zee sikh **bit**-teh ows/ahn	Get (un)dressed, please.
Machen Sie die den Oberkörper frei.	**mahkh**-en ze dehn **oh**-ber-kur-per frye	Undress to the waist.
Legen Sie sich bitte einen Augenblick hin.	**layg**-en zee zikh **bit**-eh **ine**-en **owg**-en-blik hin	Lie down a moment, please.
Öffnen Sie den Mund.	**urf**-nen zee dehn munt	Open your mouth.
Zeigen Sie die Zunge.	**tsye**-gen zee dee **tsun**-geh	Stick out your tongue.
Husten Sie.	**hoos**-ten zee	Cough.
Tief durchatmen.	teef **durkh**-aht-men	Breathe deeply.
Zeigen Sie mir wo es weh tut.	**tsy**-gen zee meer voh ehs vay toot	Show me where it hurts.
Ich werde Ihre Temperatur nehmen.	ikh vehr-deh **ee**-reh tehm-pay-raa-**toor** nay-men	I'm going to take your temperature.
Ich möchte Ihren Blutdruck/Puls messen.	ikh **murkh**-teh **ee**-ren **bloot**-druk/puls meh-sen	I'd like to take your blood pressure/pulse.
Sind Sie gegen Tetanus geimpft?	zint zee **gah**-gen **tah**-tah-nuhs gah-**impft**	Have you been vaccinated against tetanus?

Sie müssen einen Facharzt sehen.	zee **mews**-en **ine**-en **fahkh**-ahrtst **zay**-en	You have to see a specialist.
Es ist (nicht) ernst.	ehs ist (nikht) ehrnst	It's (not) serious.

Questions you might have

Do I have to go to the hospital?	Muß ich ins Krankenhaus gehen?	muss ikh ins **krahnk**-en hows **gay**-hen
Is it serious/contagious?	Ist es ernst/ansteckend?	ist ehs ehrnst/**ahn**-shteh-kehnt
What's actually wrong with me?	Was fehlt mir eigenlich?	vahs fehlt meer **eye**-gent-likh
How long should I stay in bed?	Wie lange soll ich im Bett bleiben?	vee **lahng**-eh zol ikh im beht **blye**-ben
When can I continue my trip?	Wann kann ich meine Reise fortsetzen?	vahn kahn ikh **mine**-eh **rye**-zeh **fort**-zets-en
Do I need a prescription?	Brauche ich ein Rezept?	**brow**-kheh ikh ine reh-**tsept**
How often must I take this medicine/these pills?	Wie oft muß ich dieses Medikament/diese Pillen nehmen?	vee oft muss ikh **deez**-es may-di-kah-**ment/dee**-zeh **pil**-en **naym**-en
I'm allergic to antibiotics/ penicillin.	Ich bin allergisch gegen Antibiotika/Penizillin.	ikh bin ah-**lehr**-gish gay-gen ahn-ti-bee-**oh**-ti-kah/peh-nee-**tsi**-lin
I don't want anything too strong.	Ich möchte kein zu starkes Mittel.	ikh **murkh**-teh kine tsoo **shtar**-kes **mit**-tel
How much do I owe you for the service?	Wieviel bin ich Ihnen schuldig?	**vee**-feel bin ikh **ee**-nen **shuld**-ikh
Can I have a receipt for my insurance?	Kann ich eine Quittung für meine Krankenkasse haben?	kahn ikh **ine**-eh **kvit**-tung fewr mine-eh **krahn**-ken-kahs-seh **haa**-ben

THE DENTIST

Can you recommend a good dentist?	Können Sie mir einen guten Zahnarzt empfehlen?	**kur**-nen zee meer **ine**-nen **goo**-ten **tsaan**-artst ehm-**pfeh**-len
Can't I make it possibly earlier than that?	Geht es wirklich nicht eher?	geht es **virk**-likh nikht **eh**-her

95

I have a (terrible) toothache.	Ich habe (furchtbare) Zahnschmerzen.	ikh **haa**-beh (**foorkht**-bah-reh) **tsaan**-shmehr-sen
Is it an abscess/infection?	Ist es ein Abszeß/eine Infektion?	ist es ine ahp-**tsess**/ine-eh in-fehk-**tsyon**
Can the tooth be saved?	Ist der Zahn zu retten?	ist dehr tsaan tsoo **reh**-ten
I don't want to have it pulled.	Ich möchte ihn nicht ziehen lassen.	ikh **murkh**-teh een nikht tsee-hen **lahs**-en
I've lost a filling/crown.	Ich habe eine Plombe/Krone/einen Zahn verloren.	ikh **haa**-beh **ine**-eh **plom**-beh/**kroh**-neh/ine-en tsahn ver-**loh**-ren
Can you fix it temporarily?	Können Sie ihn proviso-risch behandeln?	**kur**-nen zee een pro-vi-**zoh**-rish beh-**hahn**-deln
Do I need another appointment?	Brauche ich noch einen Termin?	**brow**-kheh ikh nokh ine-en tehr-**meen**
How much do I owe you for your service?	Wieviel bin ich Ihnen schuldig?	**vee**-feel bin ikh **een**-en **shuld**-ikh

THE OPTICIAN

I'd like to get these glasses repaired.	Ich möchte diese Brille reparieren lassen.	ikh **merkh**-teh **dee**-zeh **bril**-eh reh-pah-**ree**-ren **lahs**-en
The frame/one lens is broken.	Das Gestell/eine Linse ist zerbrochen.	dahs geh-**shtehl**/ine-eh **lin**-zeh ist tsehr-**brokh**-en
The screw must be replaced.	Die Schraube muß ersetzt werden.	dee **shrow**-beh muss ehr-**zetst vehr**-den
I lost a contact lens.	Ich habe eine Kontakt-linse verloren.	ikh **haa**-beh ine-eh kon-**tahkt**-lin-zeh fehr-**loh**-ren
Can you replace them?	Können Sie sie ersetzen?	**kur**-nen zee zee ehr-**zeht**-sen
How much does it cost?	Wieviel kostet es?	**vee**-feel **kohs**-tet ehs

Accidents and emergencies

English	German	Pronunciation
Help me quick!	Helfen Sie mir, schnell!	**helf**-en zee meer, shnel
It's an emergency!	Es ist ein Notfall!	ehs ist ine **noht**-fahl
Call a doctor/ambulance immediately!	Rufen Sie sofort einen Arzt/Krankenwagen!	**roo**-fen zee zoh-**fort** ine-en ahrtst/**krahn**-ken-vaa-gen
Get me/him/her to the hospital as quickly as possible.	Bringen Sie mich/ihn/sie so schnell wie möglich ins Krankenhaus.	**brin**-gen zee mikh/een/ zee zoh shnehl vee **murg**-likh ins **krahn**-ken-hows
I was in an accident.	Ich war in einem Unfall.	**ikh** vahr in **ine**-em **un**-fahl
I need first aid.	Ich brauche erste Hilfe.	ikh **brow**-kheh ehrs-teh hil-feh
I'm (he/she is) bleeding.	Ich blute (sie/er) blutet.	ikh **bloo**-teh (zee/ehr) **bloo**-tet
I've (he/she) lost a lot of blood.	Ich blute (sie/er) hat viel Blut verloren.	ikh **bloo**-teh (zee/ehr) haht feel bloot fehr-**loh**-ren
I think something is broken/dislocated.	Ich glaube etwas ist gebrochen/verrenkt.	ikh **glow**-beh **eht**-vahs ist geh-**brokh**-en/fehr-**rehnkt**
I can't move my arm/knee/leg.	Ich kann meinen Arm mein Knie/Bein nicht bewegen.	ikh kahn mine-en ahrm, mine knee/bine nikht beh-**vahg**-en
His/her arm is broken.	Sein/ihr Arm ist gebrochen.	zine/eer ahrm ist geh-**brokh**-en
His/her ankle is swollen.	Sein/ihr Knöchel ist geschwollen.	zine/eer **knur**-shel ist geh-**shvol**-en
Please notify my family.	Benachrichtigen Sie bitte meine Familie.	beh-**nahkh**-rikh-tee-gen zee **bit**-teh **mine**-eh fah-**meel**-yeh
What are the visiting hours?	Wann sind die Besuchszeiten?	vahn zint dee beh-**zookhs**-tsye-ten
When will the doctor come? I'm in pain.	Wann kommt der Arzt? Ich habe Schmerzen.	vahn komt dehr artst ikh **haa**-beh **shmehr**-tsen

Emergency Card

A crisis can reduce us to babbling unintelligibly even in our first language. Dealing with serious problems in a language we are just "trying on" is more stressful still. This is why we recommend that you complete this emergency card and keep a copy in your wallet with your ID.

Name: _____
first name/surname (vorname/familienname)

Address: _____
number/street (stralzennummer)

_____
city/postal code/province (stadt/post leitzahl/provinz)

Telephone number: _____
telephone number (telefonnummer)

Blood group (blutgruppe) _____

Health card number _____

Medical insurance company and policy number
(versicherungs-nummer): _____

Traveller's insurance company and policy number
(versicherungs-nummer): _____

Allergies (allergien): _____

Other medical conditions
(sonstige): _____

Medication (medikament): _____

Person to contact in case of emergency:

Name: _____
first name/surname (vorname/familienname)

Address: _____
number/street (stralzennummer)

_____
city/postal code/province (stadt/post leitzahl/provinz)

Telephone number: _____
telephone number (telefonnummer)

OVER 100 CLASSIC COLES NOTES ARE ALSO AVAILABLE:

For fifty years, Coles Notes have been helping students get through high school and university. New Coles Notes will help get you through the rest of life.

Look for these NEW COLES NOTES!

GETTING ALONG IN ...
- French
- Spanish
- Italian
- German
- Russian

HOW TO ...
- Write Effective Business Letters
- Write a Great Résumé
- Do A Great Job Interview
- Start Your Own Small Business
- Buy and Sell Your Home
- Plan Your Estate

YOUR GUIDE TO ...
- Basic Investing
- Mutual Funds
- Investing in Stocks
- Speed Reading
- Public Speaking
- Wine
- Effective Business Presentations

MOMS AND DADS' GUIDE TO ...
- Basketball for Kids
- Baseball for Kids
- Soccer for Kids
- Hockey for Kids
- Gymnastics for Kids
- Martial Arts for Kids
- Helping Your Child in Math
- Raising A Reader
- Your Child: The First Year
- Your Child: The Terrific Twos
- Your Child: Age Three and Four

HOW TO GET AN A IN ...
- Sequences & Series
- Trigonometry & Circle Geometry
- Senior Algebra with Logs & Exponents
- Permutations, Combinations & Probability
- Statistics & Data Analysis
- Calculus
- Senior Physics
- Senior English Essays
- School Projects & Presentations

NOTES & UPDATES

NOTES & UPDATES

NOTES & UPDATES